TWAYNE'S WORLD AUTHORS SERIES

A Survey of the World's Literature

Sylvia E. Bowman, Indiana University

GENERAL EDITOR

SOUTH AFRICA

Joseph Jones, University of Texas

EDITOR

Nadine Gordimer

(TWAS 315)

Photo by David Goldblatt

Nadine Gordimer

Nadine Gordimer

By ROBERT F. HAUGH

University of Michigan

Twayne Publishers, Inc.   ::   New York

Library of Congress Cataloging in Publication Data

Haugh, Robert F
  Nadine Gordimer

  (Twayne's world authors series, TWAS 315. South Africa)
  1. Gordimer, Nadine.
PR6057.063Z7   823   74-1350
ISBN 0–8057–2387–0

For Georgia, my wife

Contents

ABOUT THE AUTHOR

Robert F. Haugh is Professor of English at the University of Michigan. After undergraduate work at several southwestern universities, he took his Ph.D. degree at Michigan, with time out for Navy duty during World War II.

Dr. Haugh is the author of *Joseph Conrad: Discovery in Design* (University of Oklahoma Press, 1957) and numerous articles on Nathaniel Hawthorne, William Faulkner, J. P. Marquand, Joseph Conrad, and others.

In 1959-1960 Dr. Haugh was Fulbright lecturer in South Africa, dividing his time between the University of Cape Town and the University of the Witwatersrand in Johannesburg, where he met Miss Gordimer and became interested in her writing.

Preface

My purpose in this study, beyond introducing Nadine Gordimer to the wider audience which she so richly deserves, is to establish her place in the continuing tradition of fine artistry in fiction, and in the tradition of the short story particularly.

She derives her art from the early masters of short fiction: Chekhov, and his ardent disciple, Katherine Mansfield; James Joyce, especially the Joyce of *Dubliners*; Maupassant; Conrad and Crane; and finally the contemporary whom she so much admires, J. D. Salinger. These are the writers, with some others who will be discussed in the text, who gave wings to fiction by releasing it from the plodding mode of drama; who released it from the old copybook strictures of conflict or struggle, dramatic scene, enveloping action, turning point, climax, and the rest of the old, creaking machinery inherited from drama. With movements composed of tuned episodes, vivid imagery, inductive slants of action, *progression d'effet* (to use Conrad's term), and other methods which work their magic upon the reader. Such techniques—peculiarly adapted to the short story—in the hands of masters produce the effect of prose poetry, as anyone who has responded to Joyce's "Araby," Hemingway's "A Clean, Well-lighted Place," Katherine Mansfield's "The Garden Party," will confirm.

Yet the abandonment of the traditional forms of fiction, like the abandonment of tradition in the other arts, gives freedom while at the same time invoking new responsibilities and new problems for both the artist and the critic. The old forms had a comfortable and functional vocabulary—perhaps rhetoric is the better word—just as traditional painting had the comfortable conceptions of drawing, perspective, representative likeness, and so on. The new forms lack these comforts; there are no guidelines for either artist or critic.

New ideas of structure must be explored; new ways of describing the flow of image, encounter, time sequences, counterpoints, resolutions and other elements of the art must be found. Hence in this study, the reader may find a few terms which puzzle him—puzzle him only at the outset, it is hoped. The reader will find, as well, a generous presentation of the artist's work to illustrate the critical points being made, and, in fact, to form a meeting of the minds of critic and reader, based upon a shared reading in the very art under discussion. Such expressions as *trait de lumière, progression d'effet,* tangential structures, inductive patterns, counterpoint, resonation, and others, must be copiously instanced if they are to have meaning for the reader. Hopefully, the gain is worth the effort.

Acknowledgments must be gratefully made to many who have helped in the writing of this study: first of all, to Miss Nadine Gordimer for her willingness to discuss her work while a houseguest in Ann Arbor, and for her permission to quote passages from her short stories, novels, and published lectures. I am grateful also to the staff of the manuscripts division of the Academic Center Library of the University of Texas, for assistance in their holdings of Nadine Gordimer manuscripts; to Miss Racilia Nell, for her excellent bibliography of Miss Gordimer's early works; Victor Gollanz, Ltd., Simon & Schuster, Inc., and The Viking Press, for permission to quote from published works of Nadine Gordimer. I am particularly grateful for the patient and thoughtful editing of Joseph Jones, field editor for Twayne's World Authors Series.

Robert F. Haugh

University of Michigan
Ann Arbor, Michigan

Chronology

Introduction

A study of a South African writer offers the temptation to begin with a travelogue, all duly researched and recapitulated, of that complex land. Since so few can be presumed to have even cursory knowledge of the country, much less intimate insights into relationships, a kind of justification could be offered.

Happily, that variety of encyclopedic dullness is not necessary in a study of a writer as gifted as Nadine Gordimer. Not only does she bring the full sense of observed life to her stories and novels, she animates her scenes meticulously with a point of view functionally derived as her story moves. Hence, to read her stories is to know her Africa; and the critical method of this study will be merely to read her stories, letting the author's views upon South African life emerge. Other things will emerge too, it is hoped. Miss Gordimer is a stylist, a gem-polisher who creates in the reader a sense of Katherine Mansfield's shimmering immediacy of image. Sometimes the gems are not worth the polishing; sometimes the style does not seem congruous, in the broad mural of a novel especially. Yet her gifts are so diverse, her range so astonishingly broad, her gallery of places and people so various, that one cannot speak of her world in a phrase, as one would say Faulkner's South, or Hardy's Wessex. Her nimble imagination and capacity for response move from the urban and suburban life of Johannesburg, with its political activism, its art and theater groups, to the meager thatched roof and mud floor of native locations; from the bored matron, to the cruel child, to the professional hunter.

The image of a bazaar comes to mind when one thinks of Miss Gordimer's variety and resourcefulness. The image is useful for more than suggesting multiplicity and a teeming cornucopia of people and events. There is the same sense of a quick, almost photographic moment (here is Bray, in *A Guest of Honour,* at a social-political event: "He waited in line behind a

13

rusty-faced bald Englishman and a lively plump Scot with their blond wives, and a black lady, probably the wife of some minor official, who had faithfully assumed their uniform of decollete and pearls. She smelled almost surgically of eau-de-Cologne.''). But there is also, along with the over-powering quick reality of the observed moment, the uneasy sense of the surface revelation only.

At such times, the brillance guides the vision not to profundity, but to another dazzling facet of wit polished like a gem, obsidianlike in its cleverness.

One of the working precepts of this study is the avoidance of adulation, that too-frequent fault of the critic who "praising most, dispraises." Attention to the lapses of the author should be pursued, not from motives of malice or intellectual snobbery, but because an understanding of failure enhances success, its worth as well as its method. One may pay appreciative attention to the occasional faulty execution of a virtuso in concert, so that he may leap to his feet in furious applause at the conclusion of a brilliant performance.

Miss Gordimer's most enchanting gift is the *trait de lumière*, the illuminating moment, the quick perceptive glance of the author which sparkles like a gem. When properly placed, the *mot juste* not only adorns the page, it makes incandescent an entire passage. When not organically functional, the moment becomes intrusive, an irritating habit of the author, a form of compulsive stylistic overkill.

Another of the working precepts of this study is that every author has predilections in point of view, imagery, situation, character, sense of place, story idea, and other elements which might be termed his creative profile. The fortunate author develops a profile early and lives his creative life happily pursuing his best themes. But it frequently appears that the author is unacquainted with himself. Hawthorne would have given much to write with the "hearty beef and ale" of Trollope. Yet when he abandoned his most productive mode, the richly imaged and symbolic writing of *The Scarlet Letter,* or when he tried for social realism, as in the early chapters of *The House of the Seven Gables,* his writing became tepid, meandering, and pointless. Hemingway's profile was lyric and romantic; when he tried satire (as in portions of *A Moveable Feast*), he became gross, clumsy, and embarrassing to his admirers. Even within his own arena, the writer is seduced into error by his emotional investment in idea or imagery. Some of Hawthorne's worst was the result of an unbridled adventure in Gothicism. Controlled Gothicism served him beautifully in "Young Goodman Brown," and "The Birthmark." In "Egotism, or the Bosom Serpent," Hawthorne betrayed his best self. War and love, told with a lyric understatement, produced Hemingway's best novels; the same basic situation in *Across the River and Into the Trees*, but with the war told in an acid-stomach satire, was universally accounted a disaster.

Nadine Gordimer's creative profile is a beautifully sensitive, dazzlingly imaged insight into situations demanding love. She, like other writers, is attracted to ideas and to creative problems for which she has little gift. A useful function of the critic, I believe, is to distinguish between what is superb, what is merely good, and what is failure. If possible, he should tell why, drawing upon the works of the writer for his analyses. The meticulous vision of the singular moment which, at its best, becomes a functional element in a larger form, gives Miss Gordimer's art its truest effect. The tension in her stories resulting from "what might be," in capacities for love and compassion, contrasted with the existing relationships, produces in her best stories an irony of tender sorrow. When the tension eventuates in a direct confrontation, that irony dissipates, and the story often fails. In the manifold arenas of her creative interest, it is inevitable that failures will occasionally occur.

In her preindependence attitudes, Miss Gordimer revealed widely ranging interests including racial issues, political movements, the English "presence" and the Dutch "presence" in South Africa, the vanity fairs of suburbia, theater, the arts, farmers and urbanites, schooldays, the torments of young love—the list is immense. Since the independence movements in Africa, Miss Gordimer has, in her fiction as well as in her essays and lectures, exhibited a balanced and patient irony at the turn of events. Her commentaries, as well as her fictional situations, have shown a mature concern with social and political change. Her novel *A Guest of Honour* is her most ambitious statement of that larger interest. Before exploring the mature novelist, however, we will do well to examine the young writer. With Miss Gordimer, "young" means young indeed; her first story appeared in her fifteenth year.

Miss Gordimer is reticent about the personal details of her life; she feels that her writings reveal all that a critic needs to know. Essentially she is right, even though her writings are not autobiographical; not even the early novel, *The Lying Days*. But attitudes, interests, temperament, literary favorites, all are there in her fiction.

Nevertheless, even though Miss Gordimer is no Scott Fitzgerald or Norman Mailer, the vital facts of her life are of interest to the student of her writings.

Nadine Gordimer was born November 20, 1923 in Springs, a small mining town in the Johannesburg area of the Transvaal, the daughter of Isidore Gordimer, a jeweler, and Nan (Myers) Gordimer. She received part of her early education at a convent and graduated from the University of the Witwatersrand in Johannesburg. She speaks of her childhood as a solitary one; she read voraciously, and at age nine was trying her hand at writing. Her story, "Come Again Tomorrow," was published in November, 1939, in *The Forum*, a Johannesburg magazine. In 1949 her first collection of short stories was published in Johannesburg under the title, *Face to Face*. In 1952, that collection, with some additions and deletions, was published in New York under the title, *The Soft Voice of the Serpent*. American readers of *The New Yorker, Harper's Magazine, The Virginia Quarterly Review*, and other magazines, were already familiar with her work.

Miss Gordimer is the wife of Reinhold Cassirer, a business executive, whom she married in 1954. She and her husband live in Johannesburg with their son, her husband's daughter by a previous marriage, and her own daughter by an earlier marriage.

PART I

The Short Stories

CHAPTER 1

The Meticulous Vision:
Sojourners and Fat Ladies

I *Unhappy Sojourners*

SOMETIMES, when confronted by a bewildering array of
possibilities in a strange country, it is helpful to have a
guide for a quick tour, pointing out characteristic landmarks,
significant places, and people engaged in typical activities. If
one were to go on such a capsule tour of Nadine Gordimer's
Africa, he would most certainly encounter sojourners.

A newlywed couple, not yet fully acquainted, take the train
south from Rhodesia. At a platform stop in South Africa, they
see native wood-carvers hawking their wares alongside the
train. One delights the bride—an ancient black man, holding
aloft a most magnificent lion with a great mane and wonderful
"Van Dyke teeth," a lion carved with naive fervor and love.
The bride wants it; the young groom shall get it for her. He
leaps to the platform and at once enters into a haggling dialogue:
"Three shillings? Too much! One-and-six!" The young wife
makes frantic motions to her husband; the train begins to move.
Her slanted gaze sees the native beaten down; the young
husband triumphantly tosses some coins to the ancient artist
and leaps for the last coach step. When he comes into the car,
beaming with his success, the girl coldly rejects the gift; she
had wanted the love too, and his actions have stripped not
only the carving of love.

On a cool day, with the air like smoke, a girl walks across
the veld. The sky overhead is gray, rippling silk. The grass has
been burned in places, forming a black and platinum design.
Far off, like the appropriate placing of a spot of color in a
picture, is the red cap of an approaching native. She feels a

serene sense of pattern: she here, the native there, the whole
as if in a frame. She plucks a frond of pine needles and enjoys
caressing them with her thumb: down, smooth and stiff; up,
the sensual pleasure of minute serrations. She approaches the
native on the path, passes him, noting in a sidelong glance the
wretched nakedness through his torn garments and his red-veined
eyes. Then, a few paces beyond, she hears his thudding feet
in the dust of the path and turns to meet the nightmare of
confrontation on the lonely veld. His chest is heaving; his feet
in the dust, cracked with exposure until they are like pieces
of broken wood. They scuffle; her handbag and parcel fall; he
pounces upon them. Her first impulse is to fight him for them;
but then she thinks, "'Why?'" and she runs, and runs, through
scrub and burrs, until finally she reaches a road, the outskirts
of the village. She turns in at the first gate; then comes a fore-
stalling vision of a shocked housekeeper, of questioning police,
of further confrontation with a fugitive trapped like an animal.
She retraces her steps to the road, and as she walks, drained
and weary, the thought comes to her, "'Is there nowhere else
where we can meet?'"

A young mother at a seaside resort attracts the fawning
attention of the verandah and lobby habitués, as she passes
through with her little boy. "'Like a child herself,'" they
whisper. "'Aren't they adorable!'" There is a salesmen's convention at the hotel: "'Why don't you speak to her, Ed?'" Ed
does, and a shy, tentative relationship begins. Ed treats her as
a fragile, precious doll, one of a set with her pretty little boy.
It becomes more or less known on the verandah that she is a
young widow, recovering from the ordeal of her loss. Ed is
tenderly solicitous, and she allows herself to be waited on,
gracious and princesslike. The chorus of the verandah approves,
having assessed her sorrow: "'She should have a bit of young
life.'" One day, good-byes must be said. Ed, deeply affected
by one too precious for him, worshipfully lets her know that
to him she is like a madonna. Then, shortly after her departure
from the hotel, all the sordid story comes out. She is not a young
widow, sorrowing for a lost, noble love; she is a principal in
an ugly divorce case, and the facts are undeniable. She had
lived with both men, even after the baby. She had stolen her

lover from her younger sister. The stench of the facts pervade the verandah. All is true. She gets a letter from Ed, enclosing snapshots of herself and her beautiful child, taken on the beach; forlorn, innocent moments guiltily snatched in fraud from an awkward lover. Then she sorrows.

These stories (the first is "Train from Rhodesia,"[1] the second is "Is There Nowhere Else Where We Can Meet?"[2] and the third is "A Bit of Young Life"[3]) are among those likely to be encountered in anthologies of the short story.

Sojourners, in Miss Gordimer's fiction, frequently have a glancing opportunity for love, which becomes a chance missed, inevitably. Often the opportunity for love comes in an unlovely disguise, similar to J. D. Salinger's Fat Lady (in "Franny and Zooey"). Salinger is one of Miss Gordimer's most admired writers. The test of love is difficult and obscure, because the opportunity is disguised in obesity or grotesquerie. Hence a pure *caritas,* a most demanding, troublesome love opportunity, is presented. Often the love opportunity is seen too late, or sadly star-crossed, such as that of the girl in "Is There Nowhere Else Where We Can Meet?" From the abrasive and frightening encounter, the girl's capacity for love comes belatedly, like a flower thrust up through the Tarmac of cultural blight.

"A Bit of Young Life" has also certain aspects of the Fat Lady solicitation of love. The young "widow" encourages Ed, the salesman in ladies' wear, who has a "way" with women, but who is shy in the presence of her rather queenly detachment. The "widow" misconception is cleared up, but her mysterious reticence about her husband titillates and charms. Ed becomes the Fat Lady of the story—vulgar, gauche, a most unattractive lover. All he offers is his awkward adoration, in the context, a very precious kind of love. Because of that shy offering of love, he deserves loving in return; at the least, he deserves truth and integrity. What he gets, of course, is fraud and an obscene deceit. Yet he forgives, in the final shy gesture of the snapshots. Too late, the young mother sees that once more she has destroyed; that to destroy fine sensibilities is her role in life. Hence her epiphany of sorrow at the end, when she receives the photographs. She takes an odd comfort from his gesture, and at the same time becomes conscious of a sharper guilt, and of a heavier burden of duplicity, than she had felt during all the lies, the cunning, the faithlessness of her passion; "A tear, which seemed to have the little tickling feet of a centipede, ran down the side of her nose. Now, no one had been spared—no one at all."[4]

The imperative to find a capacity for love in an unlikely relationship (the essence of the Fat Lady sanction) is evident as well in Miss Gordimer's most famous story, "The Train from Rhodesia." The ancient black and his entrancing lion become the occasion for loving, which is of course missed by the young husband. As in Hemingway's "Hills Like White Elephants," the failure of response to the girl's whimsy signals a more fundamental fracture in rapport. As in the Hemingway story, the whimsy reveals a coarser fibre in personality, not merely an aesthetic failure in appreciating a carving or the vision of the hills. In the Hemingway story, the man's failure to share the girl's gentle whimsy shuts them both off from the harmonies of fields, trees, grass, and finally life itself. Miss Gordimer's resolution also promises sterility for the two beyond the time scheme of the story.

The genius in Miss Gordimer's vision of love-denied lies in the very capturing of the out-of-the-way opportunity for loving, the often awkward chance, which of course always becomes the chance missed. An enduring relationship, such as that of the young married couple in "The Train From Rhodesia" often furnishes the missed chance, but more frequently chance encounters between strangers, such as in "A Bit of Young Life" and "Is There Nowhere Else Where We Can Meet?" are the occasions for narrow apertures of opportunity.

"Enemies,"[5] a story which follows "A Bit of Young Life" in Six Feet of the Country offers the discovery, too late, of a fat lady who needs loving. The scene is the night train from Cape Town to Johannesburg. The protagonist is a coldly reserved woman, once a baroness, who "keeps herself to herself" when she travels. In an adjoining compartment is an old lady, obese, vulgarly loaded with string bags and paper parcels, who tries to open conversation with Mrs. Clara Hansen, and is quickly rebuffed. Nevertheless, the two women are brought together by the exigencies of travel. Seats in the dining car are scarce, and Mrs. Hansen is forced to hear about sons and daughters, grandsons and granddaughters, as she watches her fat neighbor devour fish, oxtail stew, and cutlet and roast turkey, rounded off with rhubarb pie. The obese woman's life is as richly redolent, and as untidy, as her dining habits. Mrs. Hansen keeps aloof with poorly concealed disdain. In small crevices of the dialogue, and by counterpoint, we discover Mrs. Hansen's life to be orderly, cold, and sterile. Her aloofness is maintained even when during the night she hears groans and other signs of distress coming from her neighbor. Next morning, the steward, bringing her coffee, informs her that the old lady had died during the night. She hurries from the train in Johannesburg to avoid involvement. At the hotel, with "her mouth, which was still so shapely because of her teeth," in a calculating, reluctant smile, she wired her chauffeur, Alfred, "It was not me."

Mrs. Hansen's story has an obligation to love in an odd tangency, a motif similar to that in "Is There Nowhere Else Where We Can Meet?," but because of the metallic, Maupassant character of Mrs. Hansen we feel the effect of anecdote, rather than story. It is a lesser story than others of the Fat Lady sort, partially because of the stereotype of Mrs. Hansen's character and the anecdotal quality of the events, but also because slight attention is given to imagery of place, as contrasted with the strong imagery of the girl on the veld. In that story, the imagery functions to establish the girl's serene sense of balance and pattern in her life (from the gray silk of the sky to the minute serrations of the pine needles), before her sense of order in the limpid day is destroyed by the bruising encounter; and the story, despite the sparse nature of event, is not an anecdote. The poetry of situation and image give it depth and organic statement far beyond the meaning of events in Mrs. Hansen's story. The resolution is sardonic, turn-of-the-century French, a caricature of ironic disposition well suited to the caricature which is Mrs. Hansen.

Mrs. Hansen is given another glance in "A Style of Her Own."[6] She is staying in a Johannesburg hotel which she considers beneath her (she had been misled by advice from a tourist agency). Yet, despite her aloofness and hauteur, even repulsion, she feels a strange attraction to the place:

The old ladies whom she found repulsive and with whom she had nothing whatever in common—they attracted her in some secret, reluctant part of herself that she wouldn't explore. They appealed to some imprisoned whimperer inside her who wanted to be the old lady she could never be, the old lady sunk into the mumbling, gossiping, repetitive consolations of old age, the gerontic nursery rhyme to which all the meaning and passion of life can be reduced.[7]

This brilliant insight, so deft and precise, creates life in Mrs. Hansen far beyond the train sojourner of her previous story. Although the story is given *bona fides* for several pages, on the credit established by this vivid sidelong glance at Mrs. Hansen in the lobby, unfortunately the promise is allowed to lapse. The story continues in cutback, during which we discover Mrs. Hansen as the long-suffering wife of a compulsive womanizer. She, in fact, had been "one of his women" before marriage. All of his affairs she had borne in helpless patience until that one summer in Durban. Somehow she had become impelled to discover the identity of his current love. She knew it was not one of her woman friends. She had had no woman friends since the time that the overwhelming probability of her husband's forming a liaison with at least one of them had occurred to her. Their only mutual woman friend was a plain, middle-aged spinster who came to the flat every other week to do the accumulated sewing. One night, goaded by the hurt of his departure (he had bothered with even fewer guises of concealment than usual), she followed him, found the house, knocked on the door, and for the first time confronted one of her husband's women. It was the drab little dressmaker. With a "licking flame of a glance" Mrs. Hansen surveyed the woman, then said, "Tell my husband he has left the lights of his car burning." Then, "jeering, mourning," she walked, like a queen, out into the street.

One unfortunate consequence of a vivid, illuminating moment such as that in the lobby, is that an obligation is created which must be honored. The peculiar, small crevices of love and humility which erode for a moment Mrs. Hansen's obsidianlike surface, are so interesting and so life-giving to the page that an organic necessity to continue fostering that particular kind of life is created. The subsequent events in "A Style of Her Own" do not fulfill the promise of that moment in the hotel habitat. Recall the manner in which the events of "A Bit of Young Life" emerged from the undeserved sympathy and response to the wife's supposed situation. Events then were generated which intensified and made more poignant that most interesting situation, until the story reached a development that would have interested Henry James: the progressive manipulation of awkward tenderness. Suppose, instead of following Mrs. Hansen as she pursues, with wily vindictiveness, her husband's latest, that instead she were led to explore the "secret, reluctant part of herself that she wouldn't explore." It would of course involve unwanted offerings of love which she would nevertheless accept; how much more depth there would have been than the Balzacian story we now have.

Miss Gordimer's greatest successes with sojourners comes often when the potentiality for love, vitality, or warmth of response is given not in personal relationships, but in spectacle. Such a success is her "Check Yes or No."[8] The story is saturated with the color and movement, the lustiness and the tinsel of a circus afternoon in Johannesburg. A husband, wife, and three children find usurpers in their seats; they not only refuse to move, they will not even respond to protests, stonily staring at the glitter, noise, vitality going on before them. The husband makes a scene; the wife shrinks. About them, the audience gasps at the aerialists, laughs at the clowns, and the little impasse of frustration and anger subsides. They find seats elsewhere. Smiling faces turned their way come into focus: the Dunns, friends of three years ago, when the wife was living in the next flat, newly divorced with seven-year-old Neil. The Dunns were disorganized, helpful, Dickensian. It was on their milk bottle that, by mistake, Neil had left his runaway note: "Do you want me to go away forever, or do you want me to come back. Check yes or no." Now here the Dunns were, grinning delightedly at seeing her. They seemed the concentrated essence of the circus: foolish delight, overwhelming in an irrational vitality. Because of them she hates the circus excursion even more, but she can't leave. For one thing, it would mean parading past the Dunns on the way out. So she watches, unwillingly surrounded in an eddying vitality, a situation

metaphor of her life. A tawdry succession of circus events goes
before her: a woman acrobat, "her still blue eyes, hard-looking
as the eyes of a dead man over which no one has had the
grace to draw the lids, seemed propped open by lashes spiked
with mascara."[9] And, finally, a man on the high wire, enclosing
himself in a brown sack to make his feats more breathtaking. His
foot "poked out of the bottom of the sack with the tentative,
nervous, hesitant movement of some delicate animal paw." His
slow progress, faceless, lost, uninformed, comes to the woman
with a "strange, suffocating recognition," as if she had come face
to face with an embodiment of the human story. "All that she
had sought was in his darkness, all that she had found was in the
length of wire traversed."[10]

From this existential epiphany, she rouses herself from her
accustomed state, no longer responding defensively to the warmth
and teeming life about her. Near her is an old Lithuanian
woman, wincing with empathy at the terrible risks the aerialist
confronts, and she leans over to say, comfortingly, "It's all
right. He does it every day."

A magnificent story, "Check Yes or No" resonates the personal
life of paralysis, retreat, and fear against the general vitality
about her, as if that vitality were a human constant unrecognized
until that occasion. She is contained, as it were, in an intensive
concentration of life-giving nutrients, as therapy is sometimes
given in a chamber containing oxygen under pressure. The final
therapy is the Dunn family, who concentrate grinning joyousness
upon her, despite all they know of her desperate, lonely life.
The stroke of genius at the end: the comforting pat, the words,
"It's all right," reverberate through the returning memories of
the story: hurt, desolation, cruelty. The acid negation of her
chemistry of spirit yields to the rich human panoply, the
pervasive warmth of happy bodies.

II *The Fat Lady and the Satirist*

Miss Gordimer's consciousness of sterility versus vitalism in
various forms is subject to both romantic and satiric statements.
Two stories which display beautifully those radical variants in
the author's temperament are "The Catch,"[11] and "The Ama-

teurs,"[12] both to be found in her first collection of stories, *The Soft Voice of the Serpent.*

"The Catch" gives us two sojourners, a young couple on holiday at a beach resort hotel. The nervous residualism of the city pace makes them restless during the first days of their stay. Then comes a change of pace, induced by a man they meet. They have noticed a fisherman each day, passing their little marked-out area of the beach on the way to his fishing grounds. He is an Indian, with lively, curly hair, strong legs, his smile revealing white teeth. He seems to them the image of vitalism, of nature in man. They become acquainted with him; they stand by like children as he casts into the surf. They become vitalized as well; they lose their city fatigue and ennui. They celebrate his catches, and they photograph his best, although he depreciates it and asks them to wait until he catches a *big* fish. So absorbed do they become in his natural grace, and not only physical grace, that "they almost forgot that he was an Indian."[13]

He becomes "their" Indian (in much the same way that the ancient black becomes "her" native to the girl in "The Train From Rhodesia"). He becomes more: a figure transcendent with natural function and rightness. Everything he does is vibrant with naturalness: "his strong feet making clefts in the sand like the muscular claws of a big strong-legged bird."[14] He becomes their teacher in things natural, and nature becomes transcendent to something beautiful and in a way, divine:

The Indian knew the sea—at home the couple would have said he "loved" it—and from the look of it he could say whether the water would be hot or cold, safe or nursing an evil grievance of currents, evenly rolling or sucking at the land in a fierce backwash. He knew as magically to them as a diviner feeling the pull of water beneath the ground, where fish would be when the wind blew from the east, when it didn't blow at all, and when clouds covered in from the hills to the horizon.[15]

One afternoon a message is relayed to the couple as they loll in a siesta: " 'There's someone looking for you down there—an Indian's caught a huge salmon and he says you've promised to photograph it for him.' " The impersonality of the message guides the reader's imagination toward the conclusion of the story.

It is a huge fish indeed, almost as large as the Indian. The young husband helps carry it, and when they deposit it at the wife's feet (the ancient tribal rite of bringing home the quarry for celebration is echoed here), they all stand and stare in a ceremony of awe. Washed of sand, the fish gleams like opal. It is a marvel, a king of the sea. Then the wife must have her picture taken with the great fish; she smiles prettily. Then the Indian, smiling with his strong, crooked teeth. Thus the ceremony ritualizes this epiphany of natural divinity.

A strong, wide smile of pure achievement that gathered up the unified components of his face—his slim, fine nose, his big ugly horse teeth, his black crinkled-up eyes, canceled out the warring inner contradictions that they stood for and scribbled boldly a brave moment of the whole man.[16]

But this shining, beautiful moment of the "whole man" and the transcendent sharing of a divine insight by the city couple is to be short-lived.

Back at the hotel are visitors from their urban circle. They must all go off to Durban for dinner and cinema. On the way, they come upon "their" Indian and his huge fish. He had been unable to sell it, and he trudges along carrying his great burden. The husband stops the car, saying apologetically, " 'This Indian is quite a personality.' " The two greet him, aware of awkwardness in the group. The husband wants to give him a lift to his home. Murmurs in the car: " 'Make us late for dinner.' " The great fish is locked in the trunk, and the Indian is crowded into the front seat. He brings the odor of surf and fish into the car, and an embarrassed silence ensues. The wife, self-conscious, asks about the fish. The catch was more trouble than it was worth, it appears. After they have dropped him off, the wife, deprecatingly, apologizes, " 'The things we get ourselves into.' " She shook her head, laughed a high laugh. " 'Shame! The poor thing! What on earth can he do with the great smelly fish now?' "

And as if her words had touched some chord of hysteria in them all, they began to laugh, and she laughed with them, laughed until she cried, gasping all the while, "But what have I said? Why are you laughing at me? What have I said?"[17]

The reader echoes, "What have you lost?" Unlike the young wife in "A Train from Rhodesia," the two do not realize the worth of the experience, so easily jettisoned in a resurgence of snobbery. Their shallowness (prefigured by the "They almost forgot that he *was* an Indian") overwhelms them like a return to city clothing, stifling city streets, and the vanity fair of the urban young marrieds.

The reader knows, of course, recognizing the chance missed. The timbre of this happily structured story has two resonators. One is the rich imagery of surf, sand, and sky in the "wholeness" of the fisherman. The imagery is vivid and functional, bringing qualities into the story that could not have been there had Miss Gordimer limited herself to scene and dialogue. Her success here is much like that in "Is There Nowhere Else Where We Could Meet?" The other element of success is the beautifully keyed, brittle and shallow encounter with their city friends. The encounter, of course, intensifies discoveries about the young couple that had been growing in the story from its beginning. It gains by counterpoint with the vital transcendence of the fisherman; but it also causes a resonation, an incremental vibration with the natural elements of the story. Because of the tinny, shrill tenor of the paltry city lives, we cast back into the story to place more value upon the rich potentiality of the life so lightly abandoned by the young couple. Hemingway, in several of his stories, notably "A Clean Well-lighted Place," has that same quality of negative capability, a dry, astringent final moment ("Many must have it," says the old waiter in "A Clean, Well-lighted Place." "Better not think about it," says George to Nick, at the end of "The Killers").

III *Sojourners and Maupassant*

In her latest collection of short stories, *Livingstone's Companions*,[18] Miss Gordimer displays both the felicities of sojourner stories beautifully managed, and instances of the peculiarly seductive errors into which she falls with such stories, as she has fallen before. The pitfalls derive from the nature of the genre, as well as from Miss Gordimer's writing persona. The sojourner story is peculiarly suited to a candid-camera capability; a first-impression snapshot, since sojourners, by their nature, often meet others for the first time, and form vivid first impressions. Her predilection for the sojourner gives Miss Gordimer a happy arena for her vivid impressionism, but it also conceals a trap. Because the sojourner has no richness of past (and in Miss Gordimer's stories, the past is neither rich nor functional) all must be created in the present moment. Action must be invented, sequences manipulated; and the author falls into the "plot" trap: the dependence upon sequential patterns of conflict in suspenseful relationship.

"Why Haven't You Written"[19] which first appeared in *The New Yorker* suffers from this sort of "plottiness." The story presents a metallurgical engineer, in the frozen ugliness of a midwestern winter, who takes a mistress, and in a momentary drunken decision, writes to his wife in England, "It's all off." Regret follows very soon, and with it the desperate hope that, since a mail strike is on, perhaps the letter won't be delivered. Reunion in England ("Her mouth tasted of the toothpaste they always used at home") reveals that indeed the letter had not arrived. Weeks pass, and he grows more and more certain that the letter has been lost. A month after his return, the wife finds a much-stamped letter in the mail, addressed to her. After perusing it once, "she took it to some other part of the garden, as the cat often carried the bloody and mangled mess of its prey from place to place, and read it again."[20] Then she tore it up.

The story depends upon a much telegraphed suspense pattern, in the simple irony of Maupassant, capable of only two outcomes. Hence the reversal (that is, the denied expectation of triangle drama) is predictable and the irony fails to close upon the idea with the clang it must have. The story, because of its prior commitment to the anecdotal method, does very little to explore character (the husband especially is primarily a contrivance) and chance, fate, the turn of events move characters about. The characters might very well be labeled Husband, Wife, Mistress as they go about their anecdotal duties.

Another flaw to which the sojourner story is particularly vulnerable, also because of shallowness of character development, is

stylistic overcompensation. "No Place Like"[21] offers an example.
A group of travelers, sequestered in a hot African airport while
in transit, pass the time in desultory fashion. We look at the
scene, and the other passengers, through the eyes of "the woman
in beige trousers." Our camera, with the bleak, bored lens, swings
from one to another for a candid shot, then on to the next. We
see "dark mouths of wet" as a woman lifts her arms. Someone
has fallen asleep, "mouth open, bottom fly button undone." We
stroll tiredly, we search in a voluminous bag for a boarding pass.
Out comes wads of paper handkerchiefs, yesterday's newspaper,
a "hairbrush full of her own hair, dead." Gradually, from this
bored, sterile catalog of ennui, emerges a purpose. The woman
in the beige trousers conceals herself in the lavatory, misses the
plane deliberately, and walks up a road she had glimpsed through
a window. The story fails to come off, both for reasons implicit
in the sojourner story (if not carefully written, the sojourner
becomes a tourist), and because of Miss Gordimer's habits of
style. The sequence of changing relationships that forms the
functional basis of the story, has not enough substance to carry
the burden of admittedly brilliant observations. As in some of
John Updike's stories, the reader (as a consensus of critics
affirms) gets the effect of stylistic overkill. In fact, the style, as
usual, is beautifully surgical. The *traits de lumière* are no more
incandescent than those in "Is There Nowhere Else Where We
Can Meet?" or "Train From Rhodesia." The difference is that
in those beautifully evolved stories, the situations and sequences
of relationship have a weight, a worth which will carry the
brilliant ornamentation, respond to it, resonate with it, so that
a mutual intensification occurs. The vivid illumination of image
and the quick perception of the moment add depth to the readers'
participation in the story; the weight and worth of the situation,
in turn, give justification to the intense vision of the candid shots.

IV *Sojourners and Conrad*

Such a story is "Livingstone's Companions,"[22] the title story
of the 1971 collection. Here the author's skill is beautifully engaged to overcome the implicit dangers in the sojourner story.
A journalist in Africa is assigned by his editor to do a story on

David Livingstone's companions, the year being a centennial of the dispatch by the Royal Geographical Society of a search and rescue party for the presumably lost Livingstone. Carl Church, hot, angry, frustrated, arrives at a resort hotel in the area where the graves of Livingstone's companions are thought to be. He searches fruitlessly, and each night returns to the hotel, with its grimy sheets and the stale life of resort routine. Juxtaposed to the futility of his mission and the banality of hotel life, are excerpts from Livingstone's journals. The grave and dignified words of Livingstone, as he tells of the death of one of his companions, are set against the steamy liaison of the Liverpool-born receptionist with the son of the hotel manager, a bored but predatory woman. Then Church himself is drawn into an unwanted draining affair with the manager.

Next morning he checks out, the sun blinding to his hangover, and on the way past "the fowls, the outhouses, the water tanks," he sees the path to the graves he had sought, and he belatedly searches them out. As he stands, reading the names and dates engraved in the granite, he recognizes that he, too, is one of Livingstone's companions. The final sentence brings Conrad to mind:

They all looked back, these dead companions, to the lake, the lake that Carl Church (turning to face as they did, now) had had silent behind him all the way up; the lake that, from here, was seen to stretch much farther than one could tell, down there or on the shore or at the hotel: stretching still—even from up here—as far as one could see, flat and shining; a long way up Africa.[23]

Whether or not Miss Gordimer had in mind the ending of "Heart of Darkness" her story has a similar power, for somewhat similar reasons. The dignity and strength of a religious man, a century ago, put against the beautifully comic, brassy imagery of hotel life; the flip shallowness of love-making and hotel sex-play put against death and the solemn hope of resurrection as Livingstone records in his journal the death and burial of his companions. The resolution is not brought off by dramatic discovery, or a plotty reversal. As in Conrad's story, we gain an awareness, heightened to the stature of epiphany, by resonations of image, event, and idea. The satirical content of hotel life and shabby sex-play has no plot necessity, any more than Conrad's clerk of the inner station or his harlequin Russian. The reader's imagination is quickened by the values inherent in juxtaposed "lifestyles," as we would say today.

Sean O'Faoláin, discussing Miss Gordimer's short story, "The Gentle Art," a story of a crocodile hunt says that "the story operates on two planes which are constantly merging—the imaginative plane of the night and its magic, and the realistic plane of man and his hunter's urge and hunter's courage."[24] Other qualities of the "two planes" emerge in O'Faoláin's commentary: the chirrupy city woman, Vivian and her husband, recently from Johannesburg; the radio blaring commercials and popular songs; the "tourist" quality of the whole affair. These realistic elements, given to us with a satiric flavor, intersect with the awesomeness of the jungle night and the lives of the great reptiles they hunt. Baird, the hunter, feels the awe and remarks, "Probably he'll be lying there in the sun long after I've finished banging away up and down the river or anywhere else." Five or six of the huge reptiles mean a thousand years of life, he muses.

That same structural idea obtains in "Livingstone's Companions" with the journals of Livingstone offering one "plane" of dignity and sorrow, intersecting with the other "plane" of shallow trivia. I prefer the term "resonate" rather than "intersect" for the suggestion of a continuing and changing vibration of images and ideas.

Note that there is no conventional plot in either story, even though "Livingstone's Companions" is a "search" story and "The Gentle Art" is a "hunt" story; either could have depended upon plot in the hands of another sort of writer, or, for that matter, in Miss Gordimer's hands when she is in less control of her materials, as happens in "Why Haven't You Written?" These are not plotted stories because the suspense action in either does not lead through intensifying stress patterns to a resolution of plot. Instead, the action offers a vehicle for epiphany, not dramatic discovery; the reader's discoveries are tangential to the suspense action, not arithmetically derived from it. In the words of Seán O'Faoláin: "It makes one feel certain all over again that, at its best, the short story comes close to the effects of poetry no matter how ordinary the stuff out of which the story is made."[25]

CHAPTER 2

Blackness and Its Power

NADINE Gordimer's capacity to draw upon plot, stress, and other dramatic elements for her own beautifully controlled purposes—that is, to extract from them the harmonies of poetry rather than the harshness of confrontation drama—is wonderfully evident in her management of racial story content. As a responsive and intelligent writer, born and schooled in South Africa, she has for all of her creative life been concerned with South African racial problems. She has, as a citizen, and as a lecturer and essayist, expressed concern for her government's racial policies. Her tone on racial matters in her fiction is soft, although not to South African censors, who have banned many of her writings. The softness lies not in her convictions, however, but in the nature of her art.

Anyone who has followed the proliferation of literature about the blacks, whether in Africa or elsewhere, knows the perils confronting the writer. The very history of the black man as persecuted victim, slave, or minority figure in the modern scene, is an invitation to melodrama, to events of harsh confrontation, to scenes of violence, of rape and bloodshed. The writer who writes as journalist is inevitably drawn into sociological melodrama. To use the material of the black experience without stridency has demanded exceptional skill of the writer, a skill very rarely evident in the long list of angry and concerned writers.

Nadine Gordimer, whose gift is that of a poet rather than of a journalist or a dramatist, is one of the rare exceptions. In the twenty or more of her stories which have to do with race, her control is superb. Only in a few does her art falter, usually because she has lapsed into a traditional form rather than her own poetic mode of tangential imagery and a slant treatment of racial content.

In her first widely distributed book of short stories, *The Soft*

Voice of the Serpent, there are five short stories in which non-whites figure significantly. Three of them I have discussed in connection with the motif of sojourners, but they also are such stunning examples of her artistry with racial materials that they may serve as models of the short story. The stories are "The Train From Rhodesia," "The Catch," and "Is There Nowhere Else Where We Can Meet?"

I. *Cultural Distance: Slant Structure*

Of these, I place "Is There Nowhere Else Where We Can Meet?" at the very pinnacle of her art. The central event, the purse snatching by the native on the lonely path across the veld, could easily have been a melodrama of racial confrontation. Instead, it is a beautifully rendered epiphany moment, culminating in the hurt compassion of the bruised girl, as she limps down the street and out of the story. Not only does that ultimate awareness of the girl save the story from polemics and protest, it invites the reader to a truer, more universally human experience in a racial situation.

The native is elevated above the condescension of the "victim" category to one sharing the sadness of the human dilemma. As a fellow sinner, seen compassionately, he becomes beautifully human, dignified by the girl's vision of his human potentiality. The role of "victim," in the polarized idiom of race conflict, offers no such dignity; instead it offers pathos and sentiment. The poetic imagery of the girl's consciousness—the sky like gray silk, the platinum and black of the burned-over veld, the minute pleasure of the sticky pine frond—all invite us to join the girl's sense of wholeness. It is a sense of wholeness, symmetrical and balanced in design, which includes the native when he first appears. In fact, he completes the design, orderly and interesting, in the girl's musings. When the assault occurs, the psychic bruise to the girl is as much to her sense of serene order, as to her purse and to her fear. It is a simple story, with few events, yet it rings like a carillon, true and right in its statement of sorrow and compassion. Among Miss Gordimer's many superb stories, it ranks first in my judgment for its beauty in conception, in lyric imagery, in its deft avoidance of tempting melodrama, in its total, profound achievement.

The other two successes, "The Catch," and "The Train From Rhodesia," are expertly rendered, but the racial events are used in both of them to counterpoint and comment upon the vanity fair of snobbery. This is especially true of "The Catch." The satiric quality of the urban, vanity fair group makes the story, in this important element, too pat, too easily brought off by the author. It comes perilously close to being formula writing for Miss Gordimer, about which more will be said later. So, this story, very appealing in its lyric qualities of the sea, the sand, and the strong fisherman, must rank far down the list of *racial* successes because of the too slickly brought off counterpoint of the urban friends and their formula snobbery.

II *Cultural Distance Head-on*

"Oh, Woe is Me" and "Another Part of the Sky" are of much less worth than the three mentioned above, but their lapses from excellence have the qualities of interesting and instructive failures.

"Oh, Woe is Me"[1] is the story of a Cape colored servant, Sarah, whose characteristic sigh gives the story its title. The story gets its effect from a viewpoint constriction: the white mistress telling the story wants to show fellow feeling for the heavily burdened Sarah, but the cultural distance is too great. Understatement and mistress-servant formality narrow the aperture through which we view the life span of the story. The vitality, the realness of suffering in the native family are given an overcompensating energy by point of view management through the pallid, guilty, but inadequate vision of the white narrator. The idea content of the story is a familiar one—the yearning to love, but the urge not strong enough, nor adept enough, to overcome the barriers of race, culture, and status.

There comes the time when Sarah must quit her job; her legs are too bad for the work. All her pay has gone to keep her children clothed and in school. After she leaves, we get fragments of the little family's pathetic story through occasional visits of the children, and by questioning other, unresponsive "girls" who live at the same location.

The story culminates with a final visit from Janet, the youngest of Sarah's children. She recounts, hesitantly, all the misfortunes of the family. Robert has a menial job; Felicia is married, but in circumstances that no one celebrates; father has lost his poor job. The mistress makes a pitiful offering of tea (served by Caroline, her new girl) and the gift of some outworn clothing. As Janet takes the bundle, her eyes fill with tears. She gulps to hold sobs back.

"What's the matter, Janet?" I said. "What's the matter?" But she only cried, trying to catch the wetness on her tear-smeared forearm, looking around in an agony of embarrassment for somewhere to wipe her tears. "My mother—she's very sick—" she said at last. What could I do for her? What could I do? "Here—" I said. "Here—take this—" And gave her my handkerchief.[2]

The story poses the strong fiber of life, the vitality and rich meaning of suffering against the pallid life style, the idiom of polite inhibition (suggesting a total soul anemia) of the white. In some ways the ending is reminiscent of Dan Jacobson's "The Zulu and the Zeide," which ends upon the same futile cry, though more anguished. In that story, the Jewish son finds out after the death of his father, that the black man has a deeper love for the white father than he; that black sonhood has more vitality and more modes of expression than white. The white son too cries out, " 'What could I have done?' "

Of these five stories, "Monday is Better than Sunday"[3] must rank at the lowest point, and for reasons which are intensified from traits previously observed.

Lizabeth slaves for a noisy, vulgar, and rude family. She accepts their demanding, selfish ways silently. She is not a very good servant, true. She is abrasively rebuked by every member of the family over the kippers, the failure to put water in the flower vases, and so on. The family is forever at her: do this, do that. "Wear your apron. Serve the tea." Finally Lizabeth gets away to the roof, her sanctuary. She draws in the cold, clear air. There is no one about; all around the sky is pink, streaky, far away.

In this final, brief image of solitude in nature, quiet and serene after the noisy domesticity below, we get the sense that Lizabeth's values, her worth, are superior to those of the family. It is a cheap shot, however, of contrivance, which leaves one with the feeling that the author has imposed her own viewpoint. That feeling

comes to the reader because the author's intention does not come
organically from the black girl's nature or her actions. And further,
the girl's story is counterpointed to a crude caricature of a family,
grossly overstated with the flat of the satirist's blade rather than
the point. The story illustrates the hazard in going frontally at
race problems. Both parties to the conflict become caricatures;
the whites in heavily drawn satire, the black in a smudged
sentimentalism. Accuracy in social statement is not the question.
Probably "Monday—" is better sociology than "Is There Nowhere Else Where We Can Meet?" in that it reflects a large
segment of the white/black relationship. The point is that crude
sociological journalism is not Miss Gordimer's cup of tea. The
story idea, and the story elements of character juxtaposition,
abrasive event, and realistic detail, do not demand of her writing
temperament its finest response.

Livingstone's Companions is notable in this connection for an
almost total neglect of racial problems, and there are none
with the sublime evocation of her most successful racial stories.
Only one may be considered even in the genre of the five
stories of her first collection, published twenty years earlier.

III   Satiric Suburbia

"A Satisfactory Settlement"[4] is faintly reminiscent in that
a vacillating white betrays a native friend because of stronger
commitments to "civilized" culture patterns; just as the young
marrieds turned their backs upon the primitive but truer values
of their fisherman friend. The story offers a white child in
a new neighborhood, whose mother is totally immersed in the
relished hatreds of a divorce settlement. The boy rides his
bike in the street and makes friends with an old native in
an army greatcoat in whom he confides:

"There's a dead rat by the tree at the corner. I found it yesterday."
And the old man clapped his hands slowly, with the gumgrin of
ancients and infants, "S'bona, my baasie, may the Lord bless you,
you are a big man."[5]

The boy's mother isn't interested in his new friend, nor in
his adventures. When she isn't on the phone discussing her

divorce, she is sorting out her things. Each night she hears drunken, loud arguments; a native woman is soliciting in the back yards, hammering on doors and yelling obscene invitations. Finally, one night she goes to the window and shouts, " 'Stop that! D'you hear? Stop that at once!' " Lights go on in the neighbor's house. A man's voice inquires if anything is wrong. She explains. " 'Oh, my God. Her again,' " says the male voice. Bellowing orders, he charges into the yard. There is a grunt as if someone had been kicked, and all is quiet.

Next morning, the boy finds his mother in the driveway, talking vivaciously with a group of neighbors, recounting the night's noisy affair. " 'My bike's been stolen,' " the boy announces to his mother. The masculine neighbor, a man with long legs and an "air force mustache," offers to go to the police. The boy's mother invites them all in for coffee. The boy runs in and out of the room, helping, taking part in the adult talk. " 'And I bet I know who took it, too,' he says. 'There's an old native boy who just talks to anybody in the street. He's often seen me riding my bike down by the house where the white dog is.' "[6] Thus the child Judas betrays his only friend in the neighborhood. His action has some of the quality of betrayal in "The Catch," as he turns to a crowd-pleasing turnabout, abandoning the true and the genuine represented by the ancient friend. The boy acts with the gratuitous, almost gleeful cruelty of the children in Katherine Mansfield's "A Doll's House," or in Miss Gordimer's own "The Kindest Thing to Do."

"Six Feet of the Country"[7] is an African Antigone story, a long and complex treatment of the white's limited response when confronted with the genuine emotion of the native. The white protagonists, the wife a former actress, the husband a rather thick-skinned business man, are confronted with a problem of death and burial, indifferent bureaucrats in an insoluble snarl.

The catalyzing action comes with a knock on the door late one night. One of the natives is dead. Not one of theirs, but a brother who had come visiting from Rhodesia; three days sick, now dead. The problem is that the death, and the burial, must be put in the hands of the authorities. All is soon en-

tangled in papers to be filled out and visits to offices. The
bother of it, thinks the husband. And, in addition, Petrus wants
to bury his brother himself, in their own way. There is opposition from the bureaucrats. But the white man is stubborn;
his pride gets involved.

The Dickensian progressions of the story are now established:
the husband in his pride at not being lied to by bureaucrats
and put off; the wife involved with more humanitarian sym-
pathies. The plot, in a sort of *Bleak House* alternation, has two
sorts of encounters: The first sort comprises the abrasive encounters with officialdom, resulting in mounting fury. The fury
is the more volcanic because from the start the husband had
been an unwilling advocate, with little sympathy for native
sensibilities. The second sort involves encounters with the
natives, the dignity of their sorrow, and their gentle stubborn-
ness. The body must be returned for a proper burial. But the
body has disappeared in a mountain of red tape, compounded
by the insolence and ineptitude of the officials. Where it is, no
one knows. Buried somewhere. The victim's father comes down
from Rhodesia for the funeral; and the infuriating situation
comes to a crisis.

Finally, a body is produced, and the funeral ceremony is
begun. After a few steps with the coffin, the coffin is put down.
"My son was not so heavy," protests the father. He is right.
Investigation reveals that the body is not that of the dead son.

The husband spends a week trying to unravel the tangle.
Nothing comes of his efforts; even the fees for the burial cannot
be reclaimed. Finally he gives up:

So the whole thing was a complete waste, even more of a waste for
the poor devils than I thought it would be.
    The old man from Rhodesia was about Lerice's father's size, so she
gave him one of her old father's suits, and he went home rather better
off, for the winter, than he had come.[8]

The story, sadly comic, has an anecdotal flavor; that is, the
story idea is one that could easily have come from a newspaper
account. The absurdities of the South African native control
laws are sufficient to produce many such stories, as a casual

perusal of Cape Town and Johannesburg English language newspapers will demonstrate.

For the writer, however, particularly one with the sensibilities of Miss Gordimer, giving flesh to a journalistic anecdote does not come easily. Such a story often has a sense of effort about it, as this one does. The characterizations are a cut-and-paste job; that is, they come from Central Casting in the author's file. The best writing in the story is ornamental rather than functional. As an instance, here is Lerice, the wife:

"You would think they would have felt they could tell us—once the man was ill. You would have thought at least—"
When she is intense over something, she has a way of standing in the middle of the room as people do when they are shortly to leave on a journey, looking searchingly about her at the most familiar objects as if she had never seen them before.[9]

This is very good writing. It is one of Miss Gordimer's *traits de lumière*, and it gives us a beautiful shot (a candid, stop-action shot) of a woman. It does not belong in this story, however, and it does not suit the situation; it is not organic. Supposedly it is the husband speaking, and one of the ideas of the story is his insensitivity; his obtuse, thick-skinned involvement in a native death. It is not his nature to make sensitive observations. It is not in character, of course, because it is not the husband speaking. It is Nadine Gordimer. This stroke of observation, properly placed in situation and character—a sensitive girl watching her mother, for instance—would not only be an ornament, it would function properly to develop character relationships and advance story ideas. Here, it is a decorative, delightful intrusion.

IV *Race and the Narrative Viewpoint*

Management of a narrator other than the one natural to a writer—in this case that of a young, sensitive woman—nearly always becomes difficult and unsteady, with lapses in quality. This is true of more extended writing such as in novels, particularly. But it is also true when her short-story intention demands an "unreliable" character, to use Wayne Booth's clumsy terminology. Her intention with the husband in this story is somewhat like that of Ring Lardner in his celebrated story, "Haircut," in which a story of gentle pathos and tender love is told through the perceptions of a vulgar rural practical joker. In part, her story fails because of unsteady control of the narrator; but even had the hand been steadier, the design would have insured failure. The hard-nosed narrator, whose business is that of travel agent, offers little in the way of illumination or augmentation of the story. His nature is merely part of the bad joke, necessary to bring the joke off and nothing more.

The purpose of the "unreliable" narrator is to give added intensity to the reader's discoveries and empathies. When masterfully done, as in Ford Madox Ford's *The Good Soldier,* or in a short story such as Aldous Huxley's "Nuns at Luncheon," the imaginative reinforcement given by the inadequate, biased, cruel, or otherwise controlled aperture adds immensely to the reader's experience. The reader, whose insights are carefully monitored by the narrator's filtered vision, gets the strong impulse to find out the true story for himself, despite this stupid, or cruel, or obtuse fellow telling the story. His empathy with the "true" situation, which he perceives through difficulties (carefully controlled by the writer) gives him immense empathy with the events of the story. However, if the proper tension between event and the narrative instrument is not maintained, no such empathy occurs. Instead, the reader resents these contrived obscurities put in his way, in much the same way that a viewer in a gallery of photographs will resent "arty" pictures done through rain-streaked windowpanes or old bottles, if the filtering is not done with a masterful touch.

As a pertinent aside, this might be the occasion to comment upon Wayne Booth's term, "unreliable narrator." His dichotomy (reliable versus unreliable) is one of those attractive, but ultimately disserving simplifications which makes clumsy any thought proceeding from it. No matter how many footnotes are adduced to what Mr. Booth "really meant," all proceedings from the terminology are heavy-footed and blundering. Was Van Gogh's brush "reliable" or "unreliable?" To ask the question is to invite stupidity.

V Race and a Satirical Intention

"Which New Era Would That Be?"[10] illustrates a failed view-point, augmented by several unfortunate story elements. The business of the story is race relationships, put before us as journalism in a satirical manner. As we have seen, Miss Gordimer's greatest success with race materials occurs when the racial materials are related tangentially to other, more universal human relationships.

The protagonist of the story is Jake Alexander, a half-Scottish, half-black Johannesburg printer. Visitors come—a young Englishman and Jennifer Tetzel, a social worker from Cape Town. To Jake, whose light complexion had allowed him to pass as white upon occasion, she is immediately recognizable. She is slumming, under the guise of a social worker.

He had never met her before, but he knew the type well—had seen it over and over again at meetings of the Congress of Democrats, and other organizations, where progressive whites met progressive blacks. These were the white women who, Jake knew, persisted in regarding themselves as your equal. These women—Oh, Christ!—these women felt as you did. Breathless with stout sensitivity, they insisted on walking the whole teeter-totter of the color line.[11]

There is awkward chatting, as Alister, the English friend of Jake, tries to establish an easy informality. Jake has a divorce pending, and a new girl friend, and these subjects are bantered about. The talk is forced; so is the author's imagery:

"But Lila had red hair!" Alister goaded him. He remembered the incongruously dyed, artificially straightened hair on a fine colored girl whose nostrils dilated in the manner of certain fleshy water plants seeking prey.[12]

The visit attains a climactic moment when Maxie, one of the Africans lounging about the print shop, tells of a race prejudice incident. He had been invited to come to luncheon with a white friend. When luncheon was served, Maxie was not invited to the table; instead, he must eat on the stoop. Jake then tells of comic misunderstandings over the phone, derived from the fact that he does not talk like a native. So the exchange of inverted snobberies continues. As they are leaving, Jennifer, from the door, suddenly says to Jake:

"I feel I must tell you. About that other story—the first one, about the lunch. I don't believe it. I'm sorry, but I honestly don't. It's too illogical to hold water.

It was the final self-immolation by honest understanding. She would go to the length of calling him a liar to show by frankness how much she respected him—[13]

After the two visitors leave, Jake returns to matters that had been interrupted by the visit. His eye falls upon the chair he had cleared for Jennifer Tetzel to sit on. Suddenly, he kicks it hard, so that it goes flying on its side.

The story fails because, as a primary line of development in the sequence of events, racial confrontation done in a satirical mode reveals no character worthy of attention. The accounts of racial discrimination are not more than cliché, and the special problems of using cliché are not mastered. Properly done, the author must seem to use cliché deliberately, as a part of character presentation, not as a viewpoint of the author. Here we are to believe that the blacks have special virtues because they are victims of discrimination, and that the girl, in her special kind of snobbery, forfeits our sympathy. Instead, all of the characters forfeit sympathy. The only saving moment, which comes late in the story after the reader has formed his estimate of the story, occurs when the girl, condescending within the snobbery of the social worker, "boldly" essays an "honest" difference in the exchange with Maxie.

The satirist, who is in a way a teller of jokes, must depend upon a consensus of knowledge, a common denominator of attitude and assumption. "What oft was thought but ne'er so well express'd" in Pope's line, states that assumption. To satirize the American western hero, for instance, is impossible if the audience has never seen a western movie. The joke about the hero and the villain stalking toward each other down the dusty street falls completely flat if the audience is not "in" on the joke. It is difficult to satirize the Eskimo or the New Guinea tribesman. The author must spend too much time *explaining*:

Temba was a colored man—a mixture of the bloods of black slaves and white masters, blended long ago, in the days when the Cape of Good Hope was a port of refreshment for the Dutch East India Company.[14]

Meanwhile, "what oft was thought" and the whiplash of a recognized truth pungently stated gets lost in the wordage of explanation. Satire, like jokes, cannot stand explanation. Either the reader sees it at once, or not at all. The writer of material strange and exotic to the reader rarely indulges in satire. Where is the satire in Conrad? Hemingway tries it in his urban scenes, but not in telling the story of old Santiago. What of *Gulliver's Travels*, the reader might well ask? Isn't that an exotic and strange scene? The answer is, of course, that Swift was talking about English society of his time, of class pride, political folly, vanity, and greed, all of which his readers recognized instantly. Swift had no consensus problem.

This is not to say that Miss Gordimer invariably fails in her satire. Her urban and suburban stories (many of which are not really African, but universally metropolitan) draw upon social foibles recognizable to everyone. And, many of such stories are skillfully written.

VI *Satire Turns toward Pathos*

An instance of a mixed treatment of satire and pathos which has substantially more success than "Which New Era Would That Be?" is "The Amateurs."[15] It is, as well, a story whose primary business is not a satirical treatment of an encounter between blacks and whites. The satire is limited to a white theatrical group whose actions form the story. The resolution, however, does not pivot upon satirical observation. Instead, it derives from a familiar, and invariably successful, Gordimer turn: the gentler, truer, and richer capacity of natives to be "human" (that is, to feel love, sympathy, gratitude).

The story gives us a group of amateur actors, going to a native location to do *The Importance of Being Ernest* before a native audience.

They were a specially selected audience of schoolteachers, who, with a sprinkling of social workers, two clerks from the administrative offices and a young girl who had matriculated, were the educated of the rows and rows of hundreds and hundreds who lived and ate and slept and talked and loved and died in the houses outside.[16]

The players from the outset are condescending and patronizing, except for one girl. " 'No need to bother with mustaches and things,' " one young man remarks. " 'They won't understand the period anyway.' " The girl, quite distressed, says, " 'But of course I'm making up.' "

The flip condescension of attitude continues on stage. The players burlesque it, camp it, ham it up in an "exciting devilment of overemphasis."

At the end of the play, a storm of applause from the audience. A native spokesman comes forward:

"We've tried to show you, just now with our hands and voices what we think of this wonderful thing you have brought us here in Atholville location." Slowly she swung back to the audience. "From the bottom of our hearts, we thank you, all of us here who have had the opportunity to see you, and we hope in our hearts you will come to us again *many times*——"

Like the crash of a crumbling building, the wild shouts of the people fell upon the stage; as the curtain jerked across, the players re-collected themselves, went slowly off.[17]

This simple and heartfelt offering of love by the audience dampens the cheeky pretense and snobbish sophistication of some, but not all, of the players. As the players depart, the fat young man chuckles to himself in the back of the bus:

"God, what we didn't do to that play," he laughed. "What'd you kiss me again for?" cried the young woman in surprise. "—I didn't know what was happening. We never had a kiss there, before—and all of a sudden—" She turned excitedly to the others, "—he takes hold of me and kisses me! I didn't know what was happening!"

"They liked it," snorted the young man. "*One* thing they understood, anyway!"

"Oh, I don't know—" said someone, and seemed about to speak.

But instead there was a falling away into silence.

The girl was plucking sullenly at the feathered hat resting on her knee. "We cheated them; we shouldn't have done it," she said.[18]

Despite short duration in the story, the capacity for love of the native audience dominates the effect. Once again, as in "The Catch" and other stories, the simple people are admired for their innocent virtue, their vitality of response, their candid behavior, and their appealing naiveté. They seem truer in all values than the sophisticates usually posed against them.

Such stories depend for much of their effectiveness upon quality of the sophisticated elements, however. "Monday is Better than Sunday" fails because of the disproportionate vulgarity and crassness of the whites; the treatment approaches parody. "The Amateurs," on the other hand, affords meticulous care in the delineation of the whites. Their careless condescension is beautifully leavened by the character known only as "the girl," who says, early in the story, "'But of course I'm making up,'" and at the end, "'We cheated them; we shouldn't have done it.'" That epiphany is illuminated magnificently by the *trait de lumière* just preceding it: "'We never had a kiss there before—and all of a sudden—' She turned excitedly to the others '—he takes hold of me and kisses me! I didn't know what was happening!'" In "The Catch," the ingenue wife says, as they all laugh, "'But what have I said? Why are you laughing at me? What have I said?'" Each moment offers a point of light and life, akin to the effect produced by an impressionist painter. The moment illuminates much more than its immediate area. The young actress' excited remark, only remotely related to the race relationship events of the story is, in fact, a vivid irrelevancy with the incandescent flash of epiphany. The overwhelming truth of the girl's excited moment, still responding to the crashing waves of applause, undeservedly received by the troupe, is, in its resonating effect upon other events of the story not irrelevant at all. Like one of Flaubert's incandescent moments, it electrifies and vivaciously lifts the sober statements of the story, giving them a life far beyond the turning of the last page. Finally, the story offers another bit of evidence in support of Miss Gordimer's best mode in racial stories. Her finest effects are the tangential results among whites, of a racial encounter. The racial encounters in "The Train From Rhodesia," "The Catch," and "Is There Nowhere Else Where We Can Meet?" all have tangential, rather than direct, confrontations.

VII *The Black as Domestic Servant*

Perhaps because domestic situations often lead to direct racial structures few, if any, of Miss Gordimer's stories about Africans as servants come off successfully. A further reason may be that such situations invite the kind of strident treatment of whites to which Miss Gordimer is vulnerable.

"Happy Event,"[19] a black servant story, falls into such difficulties. Like "Six Feet of the Country," it involves native death and the local police. The story gives us an African Hetty (from *Adam Bede*) who conceals her pregnancy, then disposes of the child. When the dead newborn is discovered, it is wrapped in a blue robe with a name plainly visible on a laundry tag. So, Ella Plaistow finds herself in court, explaining that she had given Lena, her maid, the cast-off robe only shortly before. When the girl appears in court, she seems so natural, so ordinary. Yet, say friends and neighbors of the Plaistow's, "It's quite awful to think that she handled Pip and Kathie—" The court quickly sentences Lena to six months' hard labor; the final sentence of the story gives us a clue to its failure: "Her sentence coincided roughly with the time Ella and Allan spent in Europe, but though she was out of prison by the time they returned, she did not go to work for them again."[20]

To go back to the start of the story (which begins with final events and cuts to prior sequences), we get other unfortunate writing of the same sort:

Ella had the vague conviction that it was best to have servants who belonged to the same tribe, rather as she would have felt that it would be better to have two Siamese cats instead of one Siamese and one tabby, or two fan-tailed goldfish, rather than one plain and one fancy. She always felt puzzled and rather peevish then, when, as had happened often before, she found that her two Basutos or two Zulus or two Xosas did not get on any better than one would have expected two Frenchmen to get on simply because both were French, or two Englishmen simply because both were English.[21]

Or this:

It was difficult to think of old Thomasi as something quite like oneself when he rose on his hind legs (yes, one had the feeling that this was *exactly* what happened when he got up from polishing the floor).[22]

Or this unsteady example of a badly shifted viewpoint:

Thomasi turned around to the young woman in the soiled pink dressing gown, the dark line of her dyed and plucked white-woman's eyebrows showing like pen strokes on the pastel of her fair-skinned face, unmade-up, faintly greasy with the patina of sleep.[23]

The viewpoint, of course, is Miss Gordimer's, not the ancient native gardener's. Miss Gordimer dislikes her white employers so intensely in this story, as in others, that she loses her writer's sense of design and proportion. She falls into the intentional fallacy of the too-subjective writer. Thus she loses her reader because of the intensity of her dislike, resulting in the abrasive, hasty strokes with which she draws her whites in this not very complex or interesting story. The defense that many whites do view their native maids like this is an irrelevancy; Miss Gordimer is not a sociological statistician, creating typicality or case study situations. She is an artist, superbly gifted, and when all her fortunes of subject matter, style, and image are in phase, capable of creating fiction of breathtaking beauty. This story, however, is a cheap shot. The structure is the sound one that in past stories produced good results: the stoical strength, the serenity, the vital forces of the native put against the sophisticated whites. But here the whites are shallow caricatures, contrivances whose main function is to be set up like stage props against the life-and-death reality of natives. It is even dubious as cultural anthropology: tribal differences are widely accepted in work groups, and not only by whites. The natives have an even keener sense of propriety. Not only does the Zulu expect to be a boss-boy, the Shangaan *expects* him to be; both would be uncomfortable with any other arrangement. Households in which the Shangaan eats apart from the other servants for twenty-five or thirty years of service are not uncommon, and it is a relationship satisfactory to all concerned.

A somewhat more successful story of whites and black servants is "Horn of Plenty,"[24] a story whose success derives largely from a more careful rendering of the whites. The first sentence is not promising, true; it seems that we are off once again on a cartoon strip of white society. The new wife, only two months in Africa, and those spent in the bush, is speaking: " 'But they're like *oxen*. If they're all like that, I just don't see how I'm going to manage.' "[25] Her husband comforts her: " 'Oh, it'll be quite different in Johannesburg. Darling, this is the wilds. These poor guys are recruited practically straight out of the trees.' "[26]

The wife had been a fashionable cosmopolite back in the States—sophisticated parties, friends in the theater, the art world. Johannesburg doesn't live up to the husband's promise. Native maids come and go swiftly, none satisfactory. Then, through a friend, Rebecca arrives. The bored woman feels that at last, after three impossible girls, she has a jewel. She tries to achieve a camaraderie: " 'It's a beautiful dress, isn't it, Rebecca?' But Rebecca has already gone to the kitchen."[27]

Later, in the car, she says out of a silence, " 'She didn't even say it was a nice dress.' 'Who?' says Hank, astonished. Pat doesn't turn her head. 'Rebecca,' " she says. Later as they drive, she continues her introspection: " 'You know, I can't stand it,' she said wildly. 'I must be loved. I can't stand it if I don't have love and warmth about me, if people don't care about me.' "[28]

The story has its small success in this final, anguished cry of the woman for love. Yet the white society, including the wife until this last moment, is a cartoon strip of satire.

CHAPTER 3

The Child and the Store

BEFORE the resort hotel, the small town store was a place of meeting in Nadine Gordimer's fiction, useful to her in the manner of the courthouse and town square to Faulkner, the bar and cafe to Hemingway. Her store teems with vitality, rotting oranges, colorful bolts of cloth, shoddy merchandise for natives, a strange and wonderful place to a child. It is a place where aloneness is discovered; where the shy meet the shrewd and adept. Here the initiates have an encounter with materialism or evil; here innocence is lost. The store is where the simple heart meets corruption.

The store, unlike the resort hotel, is a place of families. To the family and the child of the family comes a stranger. Or perhaps the child in the store feels a stranger in his own family. He is the child-left-out, or the child alienated.

"The Defeated"[1] is told from the viewpoint of a fastidious, but fascinated girl who visits the store where a schoolmate lives. We get a beautifully rich image of the neighborhood:

My mother did not want me to go near the Concession stores because they smelled, and were dirty, and the natives spat tuberculosis germs into the dust. She said it was no place for little girls.

But I used to go down there sometimes, in the afternoon, when static four o'clock held the houses of our Mine, and the sun washed over them like waves of the sea over sand castles. I felt that life was going on down there at the Concession stores: noise and movement and yes, bad smells even—and so I would wander down the naked road, with the hot sun uncomfortably drying the membrane inside my nose, seeing the irregular line of narrow white shops lying away ahead like a jumble of shoe boxes.[2]

Soon she is immersed in the rich, filthy vitality of the Concession: sucked-out orange peels with the Concession cats sniff-

51

ing at them, mealies (corn) being roasted, the air thick with
the incense of native body smell, entrails hanging in the shop
windows, blood-spattered sawdust, natives in dusty blankets:

Nevertheless, I was careful not to let them brush too closely past
me, lest some unnameable *something* crawl from their dusty
blankets or torn cotton trousers onto my clean self, and I did not
like the way they spat, with that terrible gurgle in the throat, onto
the gutter, or worse still, blew their noses loudly between finger and
thumb, and flung the excrement horribly to the air.[3]

Miss Gordimer is engaged in something more than being an
African Hogarth, as we discover when we get into the story
of Miriam, her little narrator's friend.

I   *The Store: Chekhov and Maupassant*

Miriam is the daughter of store proprietors, a small black-
haired girl whom our narrator had noticed at school only because of the ugliness of her name: Miriam Saiyetovitz. Here,
in her parents' store, she has the magic advantages of a storekeeper's kid—she is allowed bottles of red pop whenever she
likes. Miriam's mother shouts, " 'Take it! Take it! Go, have it!' "

I thought she was angry, she spoke with such impatience; but
soon I knew it was only her eager generosity that made her fling
permission almost fiercely at Miriam whenever the child made some
request.[4]

The description of the store is treated as a rich genre scene:

Light danced only furtively along the folds of the blankets that
hung from the ceiling; crackling and secret little fires in the curly
woolen furze. The blankets were dark sombre hangings, in proud
colors, bold and primal. They hung like dark stalactites in the
cave, still and heavy, communing only their own colors back to
themselves. They brooded over the shop, and over Mr. Saiyetovitz,
there beneath, treading the worn cement with his disgruntled, dispossessed air of doing his best.[5]

The mother, "ugly, with the blunt ugliness of a toad," is an
old-country peasant, as is the father. Their lives are the store

and their beautiful daughter who can speak English so well. The father is a gentle man, "with an almost hangdog gentleness" except when dealing with the natives. When trading with the natives, an angry power transforms him:

> Africans are the slowest buyers in the world; to them, buying is a ritual, a slow and solemn undertaking. They must go carefully, they nervously scent pitfalls on every side—On a busy Saturday they must be allowed to stand about the shop endlessly looking up and. about, pausing to shake their heads and give a profound "OW!"; sauntering off, going to press their noses against the window, coming back—
> And then Mr. Saiyetovitz swooping away in a gesture of rage and denial, don't care, sick-to-death. And the boy anxious, edging forward to feel the cloth again, and the whole business starting up all over again; more blankets, different colors, down from the shelf and hooked from the ceiling—stalactites crumpled to woolen heaps to wonder over. Mr. Saiyetovitz throwing them down, moving in jerks of rage now, and then roughly bullying the boy into a decision. Shouting at him, bundling his purchase into his arms, snatching the money, gesturing him cowed out of the store.
> Mr. Saiyetovitz treated the natives honestly, but with bad grace. He forced them to feel their ignorance, their inadequacy, and their submission to the white man's world of money. He spiritually maltreated them, and bitterly drove his nail into the coffin of their confidence.[6]

Miss Gordimer's purpose in this delightfully embroidered glimpse of life in the store emerges in the counterpoint of Miriam's life, quickly told, as it relates to the old parents. The final effect is, structurally, like that achieved in Katherine Mansfield's 'The Garden Party," or "Bliss," or in Hemingway's "The Gambler, the Nun, and the Radio." The story method uses an inductive process (rather than plot), whereby currents of thought set up in one sequence (usually richly imaged, as here) create a flow of ideas in another sequence, with no direct plot connection or overt conflict.

The story of Miriam and her storekeeping ugly parents could have been, in a less gifted storyteller, a confrontation sequence, demonstrating the generation gap. Much shouting, defiance, ultimatum pronouncements, and so on. Instead, the two life styles exist in their own circuits, so to speak. Only the reader's imagination, expertly guided by the author, leaps from one circuit to another, producing an induced flow of current which carries insight, irony, sadness.

Miriam's story is told quickly. She becomes a young lady, a university student, a strikingly beautiful young Jewess. Next to her, the feminine narrator "felt pale in my Scotch gingery-fairness" (the girl telling the story in *The Lying Days,* Miss Gordimer's first novel, also is a Scots ginger-redhead). Miriam gains entrance to the sophisticated young set; she goes to dances and swimming parties at fine homes. Her parents see less and less of her. Then the war separates the two girls. We get fragmentary news, one item being that Miriam has married well—a young Johannesburg doctor.

Upon return after war duty, we go again to the little store, to see Miriam's parents and to inquire of her. The store is the same—same dust, same blankets swinging overhead, same heavy, greasy atmosphere. Mr. and Mrs. Saiyetovitz are older, of course, but not merely physically: "His hands lay, with a curious, helpless indifference, curled on the counter." The wife is more stooped, uglier, and becoming blind—"that enquiring look of the blind or deaf smiling unsure at you from her face."

They produce photographs of Miriam's home in one of the rich suburbs of Johannesburg. Of Miriam they have seen little. They have seen her little boy only three times since he was born. The husband they have never seen.

Then comes the event in the store which causes the current of thought to flow between the story of Miriam and the story of her peasant parents:

But in a little while a Swazi in a tobacco-colored blanket sauntered dreamily into the shop, and Mr. Saiyetovitz rose, heavy with defeat.

Through the eddy of dust in the lonely interior and the wavering fear around the head of the native and the bright hot dance of the jazz blankets and the dreadful submission of Mrs. Saiyetovitz's conquered voice in my ear, I heard his voice strike like a snake at my faith: angry and browbeating, sullen and final, lashing weakness at the weak.

Mr. Saiyetovitz and the native.

Defeated, and without understanding in their defeat.[7]

We discover, if we had not before, that the story is not of Miriam, but of her parents. The redolent vitality of the store and the brilliant richness of the mature daughter are intended to give meaning to the ugly, devoted parents. It is a Chekhov story, the story of losers, of schlemiels, but with an element not found in Chekhov. That is the hard, objective view of Mr. Saiyetovitz as he obeys the law of the pecking order; that is pure de Maupassant. It is not de Maupassant in its beautifully inductive structure, however. There, Chekhov and Katherine Mansfield have been superb teachers.

Another story of growing up in a store is "The Umbilical Cord," also to be found in *The Soft Voice of the Serpent*. Here, too, parents and their young are the occasion. Leo, the son, is seventeen and rebellious. He feels stultified in the store with its blankets, its "personal sweat-smell" of the anxious native customer. He watches his father and mother going about their storekeeping duties: the father's "flap of gray skin stretching between his chin and collarless shirt," his mother making a little ceremony of delight whenever she could supply a customer with some item in short supply. His mother smiles at him, not noticing his disdainful stare, and she brags to a customer, " 'He's going to be a chemist.' "

"To come back to this. To belong to this,"[8] he says to himself in disgust, and looks at them "with the eye of a snake." Then, into the store comes Marius Coetzee and his daughter, a coarse, sensuously appealing girl, "like a pumpkin flower." Leo knows her, and he cringes in anticipation of what may bring the father there with her. Coetzee, a staunch Nationalist, never had traded there; he drove into town to the big Nationalist Co-op. Only one thing could bring him—he has found out about Leo and his daughter. Like the young man in Joyce's "The Boarding House," Leo waits helplessly, no longer a disdainful and rebellious young man. He hears Coetzee say something. The girl listens, lifting her leg absentmindedly so she can scratch her ankle. The mother bustles over, takes the girl to a rack of raincoats. "Just the one your daughter wants, Meneer Coetzee."

After they have gone, the parents talk in wonderment. "Did you see that? Marius Coetzee hasn't been in here for twenty year. But her daughter sees a raincoat that she wants, and we've got it, and its her birthday—'"[9] Leo has been lost in his own wonderment, scarcely daring to breathe during the encounter. Then a weak, childish happiness floods his heart. He goes to stand near his mother, and he reverts to child-in-the-store: "'Mother,' he whispered in her ear. 'Pinch me a pickle. A mustard one. I feel like a pickle.'"[10] So the young one, in the midst of a maturity rebellion, reverts to the child's role and the solace of a mother-fetish.

The story depends for its success upon several responses from the reader. One is some knowledge of the Oedipus pattern, particularly that portion having to do with the ritual disposition of the parent as necessary to the maturity process. But, as in Frank O'Connor's delightfully comic story, "My Oedipus Complex," the story also asks of the reader that he see another comic reality in parent-child relationships. The story also depends upon a suspense-plot expectation, in preparation for anticlimax. The reversal represented by anticlimax can succeed only if the reader has been led along a garden path of climactic suspense. In other words, the technique of anticlimax can succeed only when an expectation of climax is created for the reader. Otherwise, there is no surprise, no delight. It is a story strategy often employed by Chekhov, in such stories as "The Kiss," or "Gooseberries," for instance.

In this story, the reader is led to expect a dramatic confrontation of the traditional sort with the wronged girl's father, himself, and his parents. That the confrontation never happens produces comic anticlimax. Anticlimax, while it derives by negation from an ancient dramatic plot, does not get its effect from mere reversal of a dramatic gimmick; at least not in Chekhov's handling. The real Chekhov effect is to call to the reader's attention less tension-filled qualities of the events: the apparent irrelevancies of manifold life, created with vivid imagery. Chekhov's gift to fiction was this effect: the immense life content of irrelevant trivia, freed of the necessities of plot function. In Miss Gordimer's story, what could have been a tritely plotted account of a triangle confrontation, becomes fresh and real. Our attention goes to the rich detail of the store, the nature of the parents, and the youth's adolescent fears comically undercut. Lack of plot necessity allows the author to enhance life-giving elements in the story.

II *The Store and the Oedipus Complex*

Still another story of the child-in-the-shop, also with strong Chekhovian leanings, is "Charmed Lives."[11] The story is told from the point of view of Kate, the nine-year-old daughter of a jeweler. The story gives us Simon Datnow, a deaf watchmaker, who is also a distant relative whom Kate's father had brought over from the old country. Kate visited old Simon often in his watchmaker's glass cage, watching the "blunt, curled hands, with broken nails like plates of horn" working with delicate tweezers. The deaf man disliked wearing his hearing aid, and turned it on only when he knew he was being addressed. Hence he missed the first parts of everything. Kate's father, who shouted at no one, shouted at old Simon always, and not just because he was deaf. "It was a great comfort to Shand to be able to abuse someone with impunity."[12] Kate's mother championed the old deaf watchmaker. He was a natural gentleman, she insisted.

The bewildered, impotent rage that showed in his eyes—the repressed daze of savagery in the eyes of the bull who cannot see where the darts have lodged in the shoulders—before the rudeness of her husband which he couldn't hear, she interpreted as the control of a superior being.[13]

Another schlemiel championed by the mother is the drunken old family doctor. Mother trusted him despite his "fault." The doctor operated while drunk, drove his car while drunk, and since no harm seemed to come to anyone, he came to have in the town a reputation for a "charmed life." When Kate goes to the doctor's filthy house for an inoculation, she is full of the self-disgust, the futile sickness that permeates the place and its occupants. And her young heart fills with "cold cruelty toward the mild voiced, broken man bending over her."[14]

Kate goes away to a boarding school, then to a university. When she returns, after some years away, things have not changed:

In books, worms turned, drunkards ended violently, the world moved. In the small town, Kate felt, everything held back tolerantly to the pace of—well, for example, those two men for whom her mother had such a lot of time, two men who apprehended the world from a remove, the one looking through glass into an acquarium where silent, mouthing fish swam up to him incomprehensibly and swam away; the other through the glassiness of his own eyes, through which he saw even his own hands, as if he had escaped from them, going on mechanically stitching flesh and feeling pulses.[15]

Her mother has used her influence to find Kate a position in the local school system, but Kate will not have it. She must turn away to *live*, and she feels it so surely because of the two old men with their "charmed lives." Miss Gordimer is using the term finally in the sense of the fairy tale in which the young prince or princess is under a charm, a suspended life.

The epiphany coming to Kate occurs because of the fearful truth of the decay and living death she finds in the old men. We arrive at the discovery moment by a Chekhovian propinquity structure. There is no plot—the story in fact denies plot in the lines, "In books, worms turned, drunkards ended violently—" and the epiphany comes to us with the force of unexpected truth because the sequences *do* deny plot. Realism comes through the denial of artifice, a point Chekhov demonstrated in his stories, and commented upon in letters.

Miss Gordimer's story has an existential quality, as do many of Chekhov's stories. Since the girl has such a meager life-force herself, she is highly sensitive to stronger life energies about her. She fears the truths about life she sees in the old men. Had they been more vitalistic, she might have been drawn to them. As it is, she gains a compulsive direction by avoidance and denial—another common literary pattern derived from existentialism.

III   The Store and Balzac

A story closely akin to "The Defeated" and "Charmed Lives" is "The Prisoner."[16] Once again it is a story told from a child's point of view, and once more the events cover years of "unlived lives" to use the Henry James phrase. The sterile life cycle of a teacher, Mrs. Keyter, has none of the rich vitality in the telling that redeems "The Defeated." It is the most dreary, the most Balzacian of Miss Gordimer's stories concerning a suspended life. The story gives us the grayish dust of a schoolroom, the dry rasp of chalk upon blackboard, a dry, bleached hair on Mrs. Keyter's chin.

The story moves swiftly through time: "We forgot about her altogether at thirteen or fourteen. Except to meet her in the street, with the trapped, embarrassed grin of children for their former teachers."[17] While life in the small gold-mining town goes on, with prosperity bringing new, finer houses and American cars, the Keyters go on as before. Only Mark, their only son, who had been a schoolmate, seems to change. He flourishes, in fact, growing into a handsome, black-haired young man who catches the eye of all the girls.

Mr. Keyter then abandons the family, going to the Cape to live his own life. Mark cannot continue his education; he goes to work in a foundry. Then the war comes and he joins the air force. He returns occasionally in his officer's uniform, and cuts a swath:

An archetype of great physical beauty, energy, gaiety, magnificent in an officer's uniform, some germ that springs up to life from the morbid atmosphere of war like those extraordinary orchid fungi that appear overnight out of the sodden soil of dark hidden places.[18]

Mark then is married—not to one of the town girls with whom he grew up—but to one of the many pretty girls who had thrown themselves at him in his duty stations. Then comes a baby, and when the child is three or four months old, Mark fails to return from a mission.

The story closes with a final visit by the narrator, now a young woman returning from abroad. Mark's little boy is staying with Mrs. Keyter ("for good"), and her face shows content, even joy:

Mrs. Keyter was not imprisoned in the pale disappointments of her unrewarded age, her loss of lover and son, the one by failure of relationship, the other by death. It did not matter that she was old, poor, and shabby. For she in her turn held something cupped in her life: the quick, fluttering being of a child.[19]

But the narrator feels it, that sense of dust, sterility, and death which comes to her tangentially from this oasis of quiet vitality in Mrs. Keyter's life.

Suddenly the wind of my life that roared through my ears with voices, places, experiences, attainments, dropped–; I fell through in the space, the silence; through time; I found myself becalmed in the waiting, the emptiness of childhood. It was a most curious feeling; a tingling in my hands. I sat breathing the dryness of chalk; there was chalk filming the table in front of me, chalk beneath my palm on the arm of the old leather chair, chalk, chalk silting the floorboards and all the surfaces, high and low, rubbed by hands every day, or hidden away out of reach for years on the tops of cupboards. Chalk dried the blood. People powder away. There was a torpor of life as if I crouched, with secret stiff hands acting a lie, watching a small, dry chalk-ingrained hand go up to a face to finger a hair. A single, colorless hair. Nothing has changed. It repeated itself with horror. *Nothing has changed.* In poverty and drabness nothing changes. Wood does not wither. Chalk does not rot. What is dead and dry lives on forever and is forever dead.[20]

This epiphany of the stillness of death which comes to the young woman, fixing her in the dry terror of childhood, reminds of Graham Greene's "The Basement Room," in which a child's experience in terror, a dusty hair in the mouth which signals death and a nightmare of helpless imprisonment, fixes the child forever in the dryness of senility. He dies, physically, decades later, but in spirit he died in that overwhelming child's moment of sterility.

Miss Gordimer's story closes beautifully with a tiny, desultory gesture which images all that she has said in the body of the story, amplifying and resonating with previous events:

When I came out of the gate into the early twilight, a streetlight went on suddenly just outside. It caught Mark's little boy in the shadow of the gatepost, hunched back against it with one small foot turned in slightly before him, the other lifted resting back on the crumbling concrete. He had a pocketful of stones and he was throwing them slowly, one by one, at the pole.[21]

This little bit of action recycles the statement of chalk and dust in its meaningless small vitalism. Like the vitalism of the handsome officer Mark and the world travels of the now-grown child who is telling the story, dust and chalk tell the truth. It is a truth closely related to that truth in "Charmed Lives," in which young Kate finds the fearful truth in the decay and living death of the old men.

IV A Child Grows Up

The maturity story of the innocent who through an encounter of some significance loses that innocence, has been a cultural variant for centuries. Margaret Mead's accounts of "coming of age" in many tribes through age-old tribal rituals demonstrate that the story is timeless and universal. Writers from Fielding to Faulkner have drawn upon the pattern. It is an astonishingly versatile one, very useful for revelation of social values far beyond the mere events of the story. English schoolboy stories of hazing do more than recount the anguish of the young; Huck Finn's initiation into moral maturity in his relationship with Jim gives insight into village attitudes of the era; Hawthorne's Young Goodman Brown in his journey into the wilderness reveals much of the Puritan mind. Miss Gordimer has applied her own particular responsiveness to the possibilities of the form, in several stories.

"La Vie Boheme"[22] is a delightful story of an awakening, perceived through an odd, slanted angle that is one of Miss Gordimer's hallmarks. Characteristically, she gives us a simple action: the visit of a young girl to the apartment of her newly married older sister.

In an "initiation" story, the qualities of innocence prior to the altering event are of great significance. Mark Twain's Huck differs from Hawthorne's Robin or Faulkner's Charles Mallison quite markedly. Understanding the prelapsarian innocence is necessary to an understanding of the author's purpose. Henry James's innocents are nineteenth-century naifs. They embody the simple trust, a belief in progress and growth, the assumption that all experiences are ultimately good experiences, of the transcendentalists.

Miss Gordimer's girl is very much a "family" person, undergoing a mild episode of rebellion against the strictness at home, the stuffiness and "niceness" of her family life. She envies the supposed bohemian freedom of her older sister, whom she had not seen for eighteen months. The older sister had quarreled with the parents over her relationship with a medical student, left home, married the student, had a baby—

The younger sister alights from the bus in a strange part of town and looks about her in an uneasy disorientation. She finds the rather unpromising apartment building, the shabby lift; and before knocking on the door of number eleven, takes time to feel ashamed once more of her "nice" home and the stuffiness which, she is sure, clings to her like an aura.

> The door opened to the smell of burned milk and bright warm sleepy yellow light from the wide windows; full in her face it came, making a dark outline of dazzle round her sister, standing there with a soapy hand stiff away from her face, holding back a strand of loose hair awkwardly with the knob of her bent wrist.[23]

The room contains dazzle and gloom; a cavern of a bathroom strung with wet laundry, and a general disorder bleak in its effect. The dual image presages the movement of the story; the younger sister's dazzled image of her adored and envied older sister—and the fall from innocence into a grimy squalor which is the reality of the older sister's life.

The married sister goes about picking up, talking, occasionally standing to make a gesture:

> How peculiarly her sister stood, with her feet splayed out in those sandals, clinging to the door flatly, the achilles tendon at the back of each ankle pulled taut, strong and thin. The washgirl at home stood just like that, endlessly before the tub on Monday morning. . . . The recognition came like a melting inside her.[24]

Do you cook here? she asked, then recognized the tone her mother would use. She, despite her adoration and idealization, is her mother surrogate; the voice of respectability comes through her eyes, her voice. The two talk of the future—when the young husband finishes his medical training—they will travel, go to Italy possibly, or Switzerland. But the brave dream dies on the lips. The married sister is drowned in domesticity—she

can't join conversation about the new art exhibit in the city—
she didn't even know there was one.

The younger sister knows she must get away before "he"
comes home. She does break away, "feeling ridiculously
pleased" because she hadn't met him. She has projected into
him the blame for the lost dream; but even as she recognizes
the feeling of blame, she hates herself for the betrayal of loyalty
to her sister.

On an impulse she stops to buy a box of the special bath
powder her sister can no longer afford. She retraces her steps,
knocks on the door of number eleven, and he answers her knock:

"Good afternoon," she said foolishly.
"Good afternoon," he said kindly. "Did you want to see me? Or
is it for my wife?"
"I—I just wanted to leave something," she said.[25]

He takes her parcel, and she makes her awkward escape.

She hadn't said it. She hadn't told Him, I'm her sister. I'm her
sister. She kept saying it over and over silently inside herself, the
way she should have said it to Him—and in between, she told herself,
Fool, fool. . . .[26]

The story ends on this foolish encounter—that is, foolish in the
context of the events, not at all foolish on the part of the
author's perception. It is, instead, a beautifully realized adolescent moment, signaled by the girl's urgent desire to preserve the
last remnants of the dream; to withdraw before it all vanishes
in the overwhelming actuality of the husband.

V Initiation into Death's Meaning

A beautifully effective, very short story of initiation is "A
Watcher of the Dead,"[27] the story of encounter with the ceremonies of death by a sixteen-year-old girl. The usual story of
adolescent encounters with the rituals of death is strictly genera-
tion-gap material. The parents wish to honor grandmother in
the traditional way, with organ music, prayers, funeral sermon;
the adolescent is rebellious at this spurious ceremony, which

has no relationship to the warm, kindly grandmother she knew and loved. Miss Gordimer makes use of this structure, but with her customary feeling for the tangential and fresh, she has the mother as the rebel.

Uncle Jules comes to help out when grandmother dies, and it is he who insists that the family must have a Watcher of the Dead. The synagogue sends an elderly gentleman with a pink face, all fat folds, and a big stomach. He moves the body to the floor, explaining that in Jewish ritual that signifies the renunciation of worldly comforts, and lights a candle. Mother stands in the doorway, biting a knuckle like a child. She says nothing, "but only looked at the figure on the floor, as people look after the retreating bundle of a sick person wheeled away down a hospital corridor to some unimagined treatment in some unimagined room."[28] The old man settles himself and sits. Uncle Jules insists he must have the traditional bottle of brandy to help him through the long night. Mother expostulates, then reluctantly produces the brandy.

While feeding the cat, mother for the first time breaks into tears. Somehow the little act of service creates desolation in her heart in the awareness that she can no longer offer her mother any love:

My mother began to cry, her face pulled awry, looking more like Helen than ever, and tears ran down into her mouth. Helen, William and I stood still, on the other side of the kitchen table, afraid to touch her.

"I don't want her to be with him! I don't want her to be with him!" my mother said. Nobody answered, nobody spoke or moved.

Presently, she got up and blew her nose and went over to the sink to wash her hands.[29]

Later in the evening, mother went into the room where her mother lay, to kiss her goodnight. " 'It is not allowed—to touch the dead,' " says the old Watcher. It is against the Jewish religion. Mother becomes shrill in expostulation, but the old man shrugs, smiles his distress, and is firm.

In the morning, her anger over, mother offers kippers and eggs to the old Watcher. He eats steadily, "like an obedient child."

After the old Watcher has been paid his two guineas, taken his parcel—containing the brandy, no doubt—and gone, mother reveals that during the night he had eaten an apple, then fallen asleep.

"Mother," I said, "did you—" her back was to me—perhaps she did not even hear me—and I never asked her what I had started to ask her.

I have never asked her to this day. At the time, I thought, she means this morning; it was this morning that she went into the room and found him. I could see, as if I had been there, the dark, withdrawn house, the room of the dead, with the candle burning, the old man asleep, with his chin sunk sidewise into its own folds, the green coil of apple peeling, with the faint scent of vanished apple in the room, and my mother, alone with my grandmother for the last time.[30]

This final dazzling image by Miss Gordimer, a tableau of an almost Conradian chiaroscuro, illuminates the resolution of the story. It states, without dialogue or confrontation, the reconciliation of the mother, and the child as well, to the rituals of death. The vividness of the image calls to mind a final discovery moment in Katherine Mansfield's "A Dill Pickle"—also a story of the end of something—which brings together the images of the beads of moisture on the pickle jar, the red pepper glimmering like a parrot's beak, and the sharp, poignant ache of dill-pickle taste in the girl's mouth—vivid imagery which states the passion, the good-bye, and the life gone forever.

The question not asked by the girl in Miss Gordimer's story was, of course, "Did you kiss grandmother, then?"

VI *The Child and the Joy of Cruelty*

Discovery by a child of other capacities for passion—the passion of cruelty—is the story in "The Kindest Thing to Do."

This story also brings Katherine Mansfield to mind—the shimmering euphoria of the early passages in "The Garden Party"—at the outset, which gives us the "warm stupor of a Sunday afternoon."

"Have you got Mickey there?" The voice came clearly from the bedroom window, and it almost made her wince, it almost penetrated

but there was no resistance to it; in the fluid, heavy, resurgent air
the steel blade of sound slid through and was lost. Her head, drooping
near the drooping, bee-heavy, crumpled paper chalices of the poppies,
lifted half-protestingly, her lazy hand brushed the gray specks of
insects which flecked the pages of Petrarch's "Laura in Death."[32]

Mother is inquiring because of an injured dove being nursed
back to health by the family. She wants Mickey, the dog, out
of the way while she lets the dove out of the cage for an airing.
Too late; a mangled bundle of feathers lies near the hedge.
Still alive, but piteously, mortally wounded.

" 'I'll have to kill it,' " says the girl, feeling a "kind of
sulky horror."

There it was, and it was not a bird, it was a flattened mass of
dusty feathers, torn and wet with the dog's saliva, oozing dark
blood from wounds that lay hidden, making sodden the close soft
down of—ah, what was it, was it the breast, the tail; what part was
recognizable in the crushed wad of that small body.[33]

She sorrows at the small head over which "a passionate des-
peration of agony had passed." Then she draws off her sandal
and dispatches the bird with several strokes that become murderous in strength. A *hubris* of strident, dark knowledge comes
like joy: "The passion of pity she had felt for the bird was
nothing compared with this; gladly, gladly would she feel that
again."[34] Later that evening she is with friends, and her telling
of the incident becomes exultation:

"I had to do something ghastly this afternoon—I had to kill a
bird." "How brave of you," said the young man, with mock heroic
emphasis. "For a girl—yes," said another, spearing an olive on a
colored toothpick. "Women are terrified of squashing a beetle. God
knows they can be cruel and ruthless in their own devious subtle
fashion—but when it comes to killing any sort of little creature,
they're the most craven cowards." "Well, I did," she said stoutly,
carelessly; and laughing like a woman of spirit, she took the olive
from him and popped it into her mouth.[35]

That beautiful final touch, "laughing like a woman of spirit,"
(redeeming the rather contrived remarks of the young men) is

remindful of Katherine Mansfield's cruel little girls in, for instance, "The Doll's House." The little schoolmates, after one of them has said, devastatingly and spitefully to the pathetic little Kelvey girls, " 'Yah, yer father's in prison,' " then thrill with cruel *hubris*:

This was such a marvellous thing to have said that the little girls rushed away in a body, deeply, deeply excited, wild with joy. Someone found a long rope, and they began skipping. And never did they skip so high, run in and out so fast, and do such daring things, as on that morning.[36]

Eudora Welty's little girl in "A Visit of Charity," after leaving a place smelling of death—a nursing home where she has been earning Brownie Scout points by submitting to the clawing hands and shrill voices of the old ladies, runs into the sunlight in a burst of euphoric joy, knees flashing and hair tossing. She retrieves an apple from under a bush and bites into it with the cruel insouciance of the young. *Hubris* is, of course, a surge of triumph over death, a godlike moment of immortality, saturated with strength and joy.

Another of Miss Gordimer's stories of the dissembling cruelty of children is found in her 1965 collection, *Not for Publication,* under the title, "Tenants of the Last Tree-house."[37] Like the other stories, it has an oblique encounter with death, seen through a child's experiences. The time frame of the story is the summer of a girl's last days of childhood. She is thirteen. Like other children of the neighborhood, she is fascinated by a deserted house near to the jacaranda tree in which the children have their tree-house. In their games, Cavada and her girl friends become increasingly bold with the boys. They play a child's version of strip-poker, at first ending up only in giggling, wrestling, and then running off down the lane for home. Once Cavada and a friend, running flushed and giggling, find themselves abruptly confronting a tramp who sleeps in the cellar of the deserted house. Nothing happens except a fright; the play goes on the next day. But, like the girl in Katherine Anne Porter's "The Grave," a festering splinter has been thrust into innocence.

The summer ends, and Cavada goes away to boarding school.
During her first term, her parents are called in by the head-
mistress. The girl has "been an injury to the others," to use
Henry James's "Turn of the Screw" phrase. She has been telling
the other girls about adventures in a cellar, involving undressing
and sex-play. She denies complicity, weeps convincingly, and
her parents stoutly defend her. So ends the school difficulty.

However, death, sex, and epiphany moments linking the two
in vivid discovery are not yet finished with her. On a visit home,
talk turns to someone found dead in a cellar. A cold wind
searches her out.

Between one sentence and the next, sitting among her father
and mother and brothers and sisters at the table, she dropped muffled
and gagged into the dark side. Her being lay quite still in the grip
of evil without a name. The threat at her back at night, the fear in
the lies, the confusion of love and unspeakable shame that were
the same and yet dreadfully different—as a man is at once the same
man, but alive, then dead—all this drew abreast of her menacingly.[38]

But as in the Katherine Anne Porter story of death and sexual
discovery, she comes out into the daylight of family normality,
of fathers and brothers:

She was able to ask with normal curiosity, "Who was it they
murdered?"
"D'you know it was the tramp," said her mother, crossing her
arms over her body, and frowning pityingly. "You remember that
tramp who frightened you once when you met him in the lane?"[39]

Death brushes near her, and the cost of her composure is the
cruel indifference her fright has enforced upon her. The reader,
of course, feels the need for concern, for pity even for a name-
less tramp; but the cruel necessity of the girl's sexual dis-
simulation causes her to deny that human need.

Another such dark epiphany involving children and death,
but in an entirely different context, and from a mature point
of view rather than a child's, is to be found in "Another Part
of the Sky."[40] The man at the center of the story might have
been patterned, in part at least, upon the life of Alan Paton.

He is the principal of a boys' reformatory, an idealistic and compassionate man about whom a prison reform legend has grown. He is widely known as "The man who pulled down prison walls and grew geraniums in their place."

In the short action of the story, we find Collins immersed in worry like chronic pain. One of his most promising boys, one upon whom he had staked his dream of success for the Plan, has run away. He has probably gone to the city, and has been missing for a week. Collins fears to read the news, for any story of an old man knifed by an unknown assailant might be—. He has indeed had one ominous phone call from the police: an old woman has been assaulted, and the description fits the escaped boy. Still, he has hope; witnesses are notoriously unreliable; his boy could not have done this thing. Or so he tells himself, then must tell himself again, and again.

The discovery moment comes when Collins is awakened from sleep by Ngubane, one of his assistants. Something terrible has happened. He is so overcome that he cannot go on. Collins feels too the surge of fear and sorrow—at the arrival of the dread moment he had so feared. Then Ngubane gains control to say that his brother has been killed in an automobile accident. Collins is stunned. " 'Your brother? Killed on the road?' " A passionate relief makes his face hot. Now he can scarcely speak; he stumbles through the conventional phrases.

Later, lying awake in bed, he confronts his exultant joy, born sinfully at news of death, a death other than the one he had dreaded. His recognition of failure to respond to the sorrow of Ngubane is bitter and relentless. For his vain investment in the Plan, represented by the runaway boy, he has denied love and compassion where it was desperately needed. "He did not know how he would live through this moment of knowledge, and he closed his lids against the bitter juice that they seemed to crush out, burning, from his eyes."[41]

His epiphany is, once more, an epiphany of failure, since Joyce a characteristic epiphany of the twentieth century. The early religious moments which gave the experience its name were joyous, heart-filling, and energizing of Christian action. The energy released for Paul in the most celebrated of Christian epiphanies, sent him from the road to Damascus into a lifetime of journeys devoted to spreading the meaning of Christ. It brought purpose, harmony, and rapture into his being for the rest of his days.

The twentieth-century epiphany, of which the conclusion of "Another Part of the Sky" is an example, derives from a sickness, failure, or death situation. It creates a desolate, empty heart, a morbid and unproductive self-examination, and despair. Unlike the Christian acceptance of guilt, which through a process of penitence is ultimately a source of love and strength, the modern morbid self-examination creates a sense of futility, loss of dignity, and diminished self-worth. Collins in this story feels a modern epiphany:

It came to him suddenly and it filled him with desolation as startling and wakeful as the thump at the door. It stiffened him from head to foot with failure more bitter and complete than he could ever have imagined. *I'm sorry. I'm sorry. Tell me about it.* The boy is alive so Ngubane is dead. . . . He did not know how he would live through this bitter knowledge. . . .[42]

His desolation, his realization of inadequate love toward one who merits love will be recognized as a Nadine Gordimer preoccupation—a not-too-distant cousin of the "fat lady" stories previously considered.

It is, as well, a story in which realization comes not in a direct confrontation, but in an oblique, glancing, or tangential blow. The truths of life come often unawares on our blind side. Often that blind side is created from a relationship with blacks, who are so often put aside as human beings, not really taken into account. But, as we have seen, that blind side may be evidenced by a "fat lady" or other unlovely human component. Here, direct confrontation in a standard plotted fashion would have involved some event, criminal or otherwise, concerning the runaway youth upon whose shoulders rest the hopes of the Plan. Instead, the author's meticulous vision shifts to the tangential, very human, but (in a plot sense) irrelevant death. This tangential event brings about the bitter self-appraisal, the awareness of vanity in the reformer's Plan, and a sense of desolation. The epiphany is a master stroke from Miss Gordimer's finest palette, and it brings the story to that life-giving glow characteristic of her best story vein.

Sometimes Miss Gordimer's use of the tangential structure takes her into the human comedy of Balzac. "The Hour and the Years"[43] comes off with the ironic wit and the muffled glee of the French master. It is the story of a bored woman, a perfunctory husband, a family friend named Paul who becomes a lover, and an ugly dog, regarded with distaste by the wife.

The friendship ("'I must not come any more. I'm too fond of you.'") progresses to a love relationship. The inciting event is the breakdown of the husband's car. He is stranded in a distant suburb. Paul comes calling; they eat the strawberries she had intended for her husband. The pungent sweet tartness fills the air. Paul kisses her and they are "in one world, a tenuous, trembling, membranous world, which enclosed them and hung about them like the shining rainbow walls of a bubble."

Then in the midst of rapturous lovemaking comes a dog's howl of agony, followed by continuing canine wails of hurt. The two struggle up through the heavy fragrance of their love-world and run out into the glaring daylight of the verandah. The dog has been run over, but not killed; blood trickles from its mouth. She and Paul take the animal inside, make a bed for it in the kitchen. The unloved animal's passionate pain usurps their own; it cannot be recaptured. They look at each other uncertainly.

"'I'd better be going along,'" he says. She smiles with her mouth, feels her lips lift back dryly.

She knew and dreaded that presently she would come back to life and feel again. She was filled with horror at the thought of facing up to her life, of finding that everything still went on, while she was utterly changed. She wandered about the house in a muffled distress which separated her even from herself. She knew the numb detachment of the dispossessed.[44]

Life goes on without change; children come, but they make no difference in her feeling of life suspended. Now and then she hopes that—some day—.

Twice, years later, she sees Paul again. Getting out of a train, he brushes past and doesn't see her. The other time he has his

wife with him, a dark, pretty girl; she is with her sisters. "The
stranger that was Paul was vaguely familiar, like meeting
someone seen once before in a snapshot."[45] The tangential
event of the unloved dog and the interrupted lovemaking has
changed her life to a melancholy acceptance of disillusionment,
resignation, and regression to a dull stasis.

The unloved dog, with its piteous need for attention and
compassion, is, of course, another "fat lady" in the Nadine
Gordimer dossier. The obligation to pay attention, even to
love reluctantly where love is demanded by the imperatives
of decency, destroys the dream of rapture. The love ethic in
Miss Gordimer's writing is not "love thine enemy," but love
the bore, the ugly girl friend, the stupid dog, the fat lady, the
bothersome black. It derives in part from genteelism, in which
the greatest sin is to be a bore, hence the crisis of loving such
individuals. The demand made is a generalized *caritas,* made
difficult always because of the barrier of distaste or dislike.

CHAPTER 4

The French Connection

F ROM time to time in this study, references have been made to a de Maupassant device, a Balzacian attitude, or a Flaubertian image. Miss Gordimer has obviously been very responsive to readings in the French masters. Style, fictional techniques, philosophy (or philosophies) of life, attest to this attraction again and again. Perhaps this is the place to recall that every writer learns from other writers. Sometimes this is open and acknowledged, as Katherine Mansfield paid her devotional respects to Chekhov; Grahame Greene to Conrad; Faulkner to Joyce. But even when not confessed, the kinship is usually evident to the perceptive reader. "Imitation" is not the word, nor even "emulation," that gentler and more creative word. Perhaps "osmosis" comes closer. At any rate a temperamental affinity grows as the writer matures. If he is fortunate, such an affinity with a master brings the young writer to a happy fruition of his capabilities. Sometimes the writer is not fortunate; he must fumble, go through error and new trials. Faulkner, in his early writings, was an Aldous Huxley admirer; had he persisted he would have perished. Fortunately, in New Orleans he gained the attention of Sherwood Anderson, who told him to return to Mississippi for his materials, with the great good fortune the world now celebrates. Sometimes, as in the instance of Ford Madox Ford, the writer goes through life pursuing one master then another: Conrad and romanticism; James and social realism, with experiments in point of view; Balzac and epic social history, and so on.

Miss Gordimer has been fortunate in her French connection, for her temperament lends itself to objectivity, to candid camera realism, to an obsidianlike viewpoint, and a satiric edge. The subject matter of one group of stories with a particularly strong

French connection usually has nothing to do with Africans, or
native stores, or little girls growing up on the veld. Instead, it
is the vanity fair of the suburbs, of lives lived in middle-class
conformity, of the slow failures of marriages, of the failing life
cycles of politicians, and other universal human follies viewed
with a more pitiless eye than in Miss Gordimer's lyric stories.

The two collections, *Six Feet of the Country*, published in
1956, and *Friday's Footprint*, published in 1960, are especially
notable for the French mode in Nadine Gordimer's short fiction.
"Our Bovary," "A Third Presence," and a novella, "An Image
of Success," are to be found in *Friday's Footprint*, along with
some other stories of the French persuasion.

I A Modern Emma

"Our Bovary"[1] is Emma Bovary as Babbitt. It is the story of a
woman named Sonia, a "dahlia-like" lushly beautiful wife of a
rather dull lawyer named Smith, twenty years her senior. She
has remarkable, creamy skin, silky hair, a warm, generous
mouth. While the other women of the suburban neighborhood
grow gently into middle age, becoming gray and dumpy, Sonia
dyes her hair, wear strong perfume, and buys her clothes in
Johannesburg. When she is in her thirties (and a mother), Sonia
becomes bored and begins to explore the power of her beauty.
She goes on a cruise to Zanzibar and comes back "with the unmistakable air of a woman with memories" and her hands
weighed down with topaz rings. Back home, she goes to the
handsome Dr. Naude for a slipped disk. " 'Slipped disk,' " says the
mother of the young woman telling the tale. " 'Her disks are
slipped as much as mine.' " Everyone talks about her; and of
course an important element of the Bovary story is the transparent secrecy, easily penetrated by the chorus of eager gossips
who enliven their dull lives with vicarious thrills.

She has a serious love affair with a dance band personality,
and she goes off to Johannesburg as Emma went to Rouen. Everyone knows about her "dance-band Johnny with a thin mustache."
Her husband Herb Smith, a good friend of the family, confesses
that he had considered divorcing her. But he does not, and he
becomes something of a hero for his forbearance. The dance-

band Johnny goes on to another town and another woman; Sonia is seen about town, now getting fat, and not a little over-dressed, the observing ladies agree. She and Herbert go to Rotary conventions and make the social pages with a trip to South America. Then Herb dies. Sonia, left well-off, lives on much as she had before.

We last hear of Sonia when the mother of the narrator wants to go visit her, showing off the latest grandchild. Sonia is fail-ing—heart disease? Cancer? We don't know; she is just failing, like any other aged woman. She wants old friends to come visit her and talk about grandchildren. Then she is dead, with a tremendous funeral, and fond memories from those who knew her as a beautiful young woman. Says father:

"It's been a trying day for your mother, she's lying down. You heard about Sonia? Poor girl. Well, it was a mercy, really. What a tremendous funeral; took your mother and me half an hour to get the car away, afterwards. Yes; I remember her when she was seventeen. Naturally, your mother's upset; when you see old friends go. . . . Poor girl. She was beautiful, you know, you wouldn't believe it. . . ."[2]

The story, as the title suggests, plays against the acrid pathos of Flaubert's famous Emma, with its severe retribution for her vagaries, and her black vomit at the end. Like John O'Hara's excellent story, "Imagine Kissing Pete," it plays echo patterns against the reader's memories and expectations: dramatic cli-maxes, violence, suicides, and other melodrama. Instead, life goes on with an effect of understatement; children are born and grow up (O'Hara's story ends with his jazz-age parents holding hands and weeping as their son is given honors at commence-ment); and finally death comes, much the same for the sinner as for the saint. No disgrace, no ugliness, and our final memory of Sonia is through Mother: " 'What two women usually talk about—their home, their children.' "

Flaubert achieved his effects, in part, by playing against a current romanticism and sentimentalism; by spelling out sordid domestic realism and the boredom that comes even to adulterous affairs. Miss Gordimer achieves her considerable success by playing off her own sort of understated satire against our Flau-

bertian expectations. One element in Flaubert's success not found
in this story is the dazzling nature imagery, often amounting to
incandescent epiphany; Flaubert's use of the imagery was to
counterpoint visions of beauty with the squalid realism man
achieves through his folly. Miss Gordimer is fully aware of that
quality in Flaubert's writing, and at times uses such imagery
with stunning success. That she left it out of Sonia's story indi-
cates her concern with other purposes—for example, the desire
to achieve an effect of understated satiric realism. She did not
want to plant in the reader's mind an image of potential beauty
and harmony as she did in "Is There Nowhere Else Where We
Can Meet?" or other stories with lyric possibilities.

II A French Novella

Another story with another sort of French connection in the
same collection is "An Image of Success," Miss Gordimer's
only attempt at the novella. Like "Our Bovary," it is a life-cycle
story, the story of another sort of Babbitt, this time a middle-aged,
prosperous businessman resembling Sinclair Lewis's famous
figure.

Charles Butters is respectable and prudent, an image of success. He owns a chain of hotels, a sheep farm, is a director in
a chrome mine, and drives an American car. One late afternoon,
the young man telling the story, a junior member of a law firm,
is required to take some legal papers to Mr. Butters. The hour
is late, the young man is uneasy about a date, and Mr. Butters
offers him a lift to his destination. Contrite and somewhat
amused, Mr. Butters then offers to drive the young man, his
friend and their two young ladies to their party at a roadhouse
north of town.

On the way, a moment of epiphany occurs, for a purpose not
found in "Our Bovary." It is much like that moment in *Madame
Bovary* when Charles Bovary stands at the gate of the farm
with Emma. The rain is just over, the sun comes out, and a
crystal drop strikes the lavender silk umbrella Emma hold over
her head. The silk, the crystal drop thrumming on the lavender,
the girl in a translucent vision of loveliness creates a time-
stopping moment for Charles. He is enchanted; his life takes
a new course.

Here, the Transvaal countryside is in autumnal flower. Alongside the road are drifts of pink and white cosmos. June, one of the pretty girls, whispers, " 'Oh, isn't it lovely. I wish I could just pick and pick.' " Charles Butters turns to her with a smile, "an uncle who is determined that his treat-day shall lack nothing." He stops, the girl steps out into the swathe of flowers.

The rest of us waited in the car; yet the cool emptiness of the veld, a plain divided alternately by the rich pile of afterflow and the sunken green of shadow, entered into us. We stopped talking. The cars ripped by on our right. On the left, a few yards from the road, the girl moved through the waist-high flowers like a woman in an enormous, rustling skirt. She picked and picked, stooping with the little pendant she wore hanging away from and then, as she rose to smile at us, falling back on the thin tender place, ribbed like sand with her bones, that, since her breasts were so small, she had instead of a hollow between them.[3]

Back in the car, the flowers (and the girl) have lost their enchantment. The stems are long and weedy, the colors are washed out, close up the girl is once more an ordinary village girl.

But not to Mr. Butters. A week later, he offers to take the four out to dinner, a transparent action to the young lawyer telling the story. He takes them to an expensive hotel for dinner, and they sit awkwardly, an uneasy embarrassment holding them all.

Then after that, Mr. Butters manages his own liaison with June. Three weeks pass, and the slide to ruin begins its perceptible movement. Butters wants to divorce hs wife and marry June Williams. He quarrels with the senior members of the law firm over his plan, and asks the junior member to take over his legal affairs, including divorce. After being reassured by the senior member that this is the only way to keep the business in the firm, the young lawyer reluctantly assents. Not only is he troubled by the problem of law-firm tact, he resents another kind of breach of propriety. Mr. Butters's action amounts, in a way, to an invasion of youthful prerogatives. Even though he has no romantic interest in little June, she belongs to a certain phase of his youth, of which he's jealous.

I felt unaccountably sad and resentful; a strange, becalmed state. What might have been expected to astound me—the spectacle of a middle-aged, solid man ready to throw over his established life for a poor little girl young enough to be his daughter—glanced off my mind. An event finds a different target in each of those whom it concerns; this was a direct hit upon the nerve of my adulthood: that state of accepted compromises with moral and social mores that marks the boy from the man. Charles Butters was stretching out his hand and taking what had been agreed (between myself and that order of society in which I wanted my place) must be foregone: that small, sweet, wild apple that was not for daily consumption.[4]

Butters's wife gives him no trouble about the divorce—she is quite businesslike about the property settlement of course, and Butters is quite generous—and the only hitch to the marriage involves June's parents. Their small house has a "Jesus Saves" placard in the front window. It is not the age difference they object to; it is that Butters owns several hotels where liquor is served. Their daughter cannot marry one who trades in spirits. So Butters sells his hotels.

Our young narrator has a last encounter with June before her marriage, a chance encounter on the postoffice steps, "the last time I should speak to her in the context of McDonald's Drift." (McDonald's Drift was the name of the favored roadhouse.) In a scene reminiscent of Conrad's *Chance* (the forlorn Flora has a street encounter with Marlow and is sweetly bereft, lost, appealing) the two talk:

"Are you really going to marry him?" And she said, caught in the dreamlike honesty of the off-guard moment between us, "He's so kind. He's so wonderful to me, what can I do?" We saw his generosity, his kindness and consideration—an enormous parcel that had been delivered into her hands that had been small and empty— destined for the typewriter, and had not expected any sort of abundance to rest in them.

I could not help being surprised to see that she looked just as I had thought she looked; when something extraordinary happens to someone he's always thought of as ordinary, one feels one must have missed some clue that was there all the time. I saw the pendant on her neck, just as it had been the day she bent picking cosmos on the Pretoria Road.[5]

So they are married. Two children come quickly. Butters has lost his business touch, however. He sells, he buys, he takes precarious fliers. Nine years after the marriage to June he is bankrupt. His failure makes him paranoic. He sleeps with a gun under his pillow and prowls about the house at night looking for intruders.

June comes to the law offices, frightened and still shy. It finally emerges that she wishes to discuss divorce. She still gives the impression of being one of life's windfalls, a bit plumper, not quite thirty. Butters is weary, reasonable:

"She'd be all right, if it weren't for me." He shook his head and his hands opened slowly and rested, lax, on the chair arms.

"You don't want her to stay," I said, afraid to make it a question.

He was not listening to me. "How charming she was, eh, that afternoon."

I remembered it too, suddenly very clearly, the stop by the roadside and the girl picking flowers.[6]

June gets the divorce, custody of the children, and modest child-support payments from the dwindling investments.

Butters turns up some time later as a bartender. Then he disappears. From time to time, requests come in for the loan of ten pounds, or five, always with the embarrassed air of one temporarily down on his luck. The letters come from Cape Town, or Durban, or other towns in South Africa.

Then, some years later, Butters appears with a woman he wants to marry, obviously a prostitute; and he would like the loan of five pounds. He has the look of a man worn down, burned by the sun, shabby. The street-walker, a month later, walks in to announce that he is dead, and what should she do? She and the lawyer are the only ones at the graveside.

As the lawyer drives back to the city, he reflects with resentment the lesson Butters has forced upon him: the puny protection, the small barrier to misfortune offered by money, status, property. But more than this uneasy thought there is another. Somehow, this middle-aged adventurer, this invader of youth's arena, had become the custodian of his own youth. While he lived, the lawyer was young. With him gone, the grayness of age creeps closer. As he thinks these morbid thoughts, he looks

out the window of his car and sees, once more, a vast pink and
white undulation of cosmos in bloom.

Père Goriot without the daughters? *Babbitt* with no redeeming
American pattern of the man who comes back, after his fling?
Perhaps a little of both. Yet in Miss Gordimer's *novella* is something more than satire, something more than acrid objectivity.
The image which closes the story, recalling the girl in the field
of flowers, gives vitality to the dream. Here is, finally, no grind-
ing realism which destroys a once-prosperous man. Nor is there
the misanthropy of Flaubert or Balzac. Butters is seen pitilessly
and clearly, but his story is gently told. The author does not
gloat over his downfall, as Flaubert does over Emma at the
last, perhaps because she is scoring no points against society.
Her sympathy saves her from the abrasive scorn of *Babbitt* for
middle class materialism. Her tone is compassionate. Her target
is folly but her tone is quiet and ironic. And we must remember
that the narrator who regrets the end of Butters does so with
a sigh, for somehow it means the burial of his own youth. The
ending of the story creates for me the same feeling as the ending
of the Allan Seager story, "This Town and Salamanca," also
the story of the end of something, and that something containing the surrogate youth of the narrator.

Miss Gordimer's novella does not, however come off with
the mastery we have come to expect from reading her shorter
works. It is overlong, it is tedious in its development of Butters's
life cycle, and it is for much of its length, a boring scenario.
The trick is to write about tedious and boring events without
becoming boring and tedious to the reader. The author is perhaps too much taken by the pace of *Père Goriot* or similar tales
done in the mode of French naturalism; life grinds along, so
the style must grind along. Balzac and Zola were suited to that
mode; but Miss Gordimer's best mode is the lyric and the vividly
impressionistic.

III   *French Anecdotes*

The stories in the collection published under the title, *Six
Feet of the Country* include a number in the French mode, and
they are for the most part more successful than the account of

Mr. Butters's decline and fall—perhaps because they are shorter, pithy, economical. The satirical tale, after all, is somewhat like a comic story. It is anecdotal; it should make its point quickly with good timing, then stop. *Vanity Fair*, for example, is a series of anecdotes, each one fairly complete in itself.

"Out of Season"[7] is one such, a story of "The Women," or "The Group." We are in Johannesburg, with a well-to-do class of women, "The Dollies, Carries, Lotties of the twenties," now all in their forties. The story is being told by Lottie:

apparently I am one of these women who have always been resigned to the limitation of their lot. The fact that I use the word "lot," connoting life as something apportioned, arbitrarily limited at different levels for individual beings, will tell you all about me. I am the kind known as "a wonderful person"—person, mark you, not woman, for that might suggest a splendid femininity, something enviable.[8]

Lottie, despite her air of humility and self-depreciation, is quite capable, we discover, of the acerbic wit of the satirist and glee, perhaps compensatory, at another's downfall. She has, as well, the sense of absolute rectitude associated with the satiric posture. The satirist, we need to remind ourselves, is not a determinist or social scientist, much less a relativist. He is a moral absolutist, keenly attuned to the proper attitudes, the proper demeanor, the proper station for all within range of his measuring (and evaluating) eye.

Our subject under observation in this story is Caroline, one of the group. Caroline has everything; everyone likes her. Of all the women in their little set, Caroline has worn the best: her hair, her skin, her lovely hands, her clothing, all suggest a serene beauty with a happy life style, at ease with herself and with the world.

At twenty, Caroline had married a man fourteen years her senior. After two sons and some years of happiness and ease, she had been left a rather young, well-to-do widow. She took several lovers everyone knew about, with no lingering attachments, except for one, the most recent. This was a youngish Canadian, a Cambridge man who had sailed in exotic seas and done other adventuresome things while at the same time managing a rather substantial career in business. He had, in time,

gone back to Canada. Then, six months prior to the luncheon
with the group which forms the action event of the story, he
had returned, had married Caroline, and was now off in some
interesting place on a business trip.

At the luncheon, the women, who had not been together for
awhile, compare notes on husbands, children, their lives. Caroline is generously responsive to their accounts, but detached in
manner. Actually she seems withdrawn from her old friends and
her old way of life. She is in love and her thoughts are elsewhere; her manner is self-conscious, transparently role-playing
in her responses:

I thought that I detected her consciousness of this in her
disbelieving tone, her look of innocence, and I found something
rather touching in the embarrassment at the back of the subterfuge;
Caroline, at forty-seven thought it might seem a little ridiculous to
let the old friends of her girlhood and first marriage realize that
she had gone through all over again, out of season, that period of
withdrawal from the world that comes at the beginning of life with
the beloved.[9]

The talk turns to Caroline's Gideon, in Rhodesia on his business
trip. Caroline's neck turns slightly pink as she retails bits from
his letters—how he is being strenuously entertained, and how
well business is going. She goes to ring for a servant, and lingers
at the wall, unwilling to let go of the topic which pleases her
so much.

A servant appears with a bundle of letters. One is from
Gideon—"D'you mind if I have a quick look?" They all make
the appropriate cries of disclaimer, then watch her face as she
reads. She rewards them, reading:

"Then in the evening we swam, and the sky was smoky with
pink light—can't describe it. Little night club on Saturday also very
good, rather drunken. And the business side goes on swimmingly. I
really was wise to come; personal contact is the thing. We'll come
again together in September. I miss you terribly and I want you
in my arms—" Caroline broke off, giving a little guilty, dismissing
shrug, a giggle.[10]

The denouement comes when Lottie, in the midst of the luncheon, suffers one of her attacks of hay fever, and must go to the living room for her handbag and her pills. She sees Caroline's letter lying open, and cannot resist an impulse to let her eyes follow a few lines. The concluding sentences have to do with business and the plan of return. Not to be found on the page is "I miss you terribly and I want you in my arms." Lottie returns to the dining room, to Caroline's lovely face, only a little eroded by the lines fanning from the corners of the eyes, now turned toward her, "Darling, are you all right?"

The anecdote, de Maupassant punch line and all, is succinctly over. And, the satirist's implicit moral judgment may be discovered without too much effort: "Every man (and every woman) to his proper season." The trouble with anecdotal stories is that the trick ending, the punch line, throws in the shade all other good qualities that might otherwise be noticed. Subtle meanings are drowned in the roar of laughter (or the titters) derived from the joke.

"Out of Season" is a tidy, competent, rather contrived anecdotal story. The narrator is partly at fault for the commonplaceness of the telling; she has none of the appealing, odd slants that Miss Gordimer knows how to use. Yet, as a derivative of the French connection, it is an acceptable story, a comfortable story that "goes somewhere" and that is what we expect of the de Maupassant story. But it is no "Train from Rhodesia" or "A Bit of Young Life," or "Is There Nowhere Else Where We Can Meet?"

Another variant of the de Maupassant mode, this time with an O. Henry gimmick, is to be seen in "The White Goddess and the Mealie Question."[11] The story is told from the point of view of a Johannesburg woman, the wife of an emigrant from Austria, now the proprietor of a marginal art and antique shop. Kurt is a lovable but weak man, who "looked, when I met him, like a great clumsy spaniel who, as a treat, has just been allowed into the living room." Others in the story are D. B. Lansdorf, an aged, left-over giant in the art world, now a fragile, appealing friend of the family. He is given to dialectical lectures under such titles as "Kant and the Mealie Question." Hence the title of the story, a family joke, fondly told, of

D. B.'s predilection for prestigious labels. Another "character"
is a white porcelain figure of a Chinese goddess. Returning from
the hospital and the birth of a baby, the wife finds a favorite
antique desk disappeared, and in its place a two-foot figure.
She hates it at once; Kurt adores it.

When, one morning, the porcelain goddess is discovered
with the head broken off (a servant is presumed the culprit),
he is broken-hearted in the real lover's sense:

My poor Kurt was heartbroken. Not angry, simply heartbroken
the way a man is heartbroken who finds that a woman whom he
worships has been unfaithful to him. The figure had been perfection
to him, his white goddess, and by losing perfection it affronted and
disillusioned him.[12]

While this broken love affair is still unhealed, another figure
enters the story: Clara Ledbetter. She is an aggressive, man-
nish woman who paints, talks art theory interminably, and
trades in antiques. Clara is not a woman to be jealous of in
the ordinary sense. But she strides in, talks, dominates with
a condescending glance at the little wife, and absorbs Kurt
completely. The two spend hours discussing aesthetics, art, life,
while the wife goes about her domestic duties. Clara, as well,
has a shrewed eye for art objects and antiques, and one by
one cherished and valuable items disappear, usually "paid for"
by one of Clara's atrocious paintings. Kurt is dazzled, completely convinced that she is a "find" and that he is fortunate
to have her work while she is an unknown.

The wife gives up trying to convince Kurt that Clara's
paintings are a pompous fraud, and that she herself is an
overbearing pretense. Clara's appearance becomes the cue for
the wife to take her infant, the pram, and seek the wintry air.
One cold Saturday afternoon, when she comes in from her
stroll of escapism, she finds Kurt all smiles. "Clara's gone."
And, gone for good—but not without leaving one of her
hideous paintings. In trade for what? The wife is thrown first
into a giggling spell and then into tears of relief with Kurt's
announcement that the white goddess was the trade. Happiness
and serenity in the household once more, at least for several
months.

Then the phone rings. It is D. B. Landsdorf, back in Johannesburg from a visit to Cape Town. And, he brings a present, an art treasure. Readers of de Maupassant and O. Henry will not be surprised to learn that it is the Chinese white goddess, picked up as a great find in Cape Town and brought as a precious gift—a high price, he had to borrow half the money—presented with trembling excitement.

A story which smacks of anecdote may be redeemed by sheer writing art, quite apart from the gimmick, as O. Henry's "The Gift of the Magi" is redeemed by the warm realism and the appealing comic sense that O. Henry gave to the young, very much in love and self-sacrificing husband and wife; de Maupassant's stories with trick, or gimmick endings are redeemed by his stiletto-like commentaries upon the foibles of society. It might be said that Miss Gordimer's story is redeemed from something that might have appeared in an old *Collier's* or *Liberty* (on the short-short feature page) by her fondly done characterizations of Kurt and old D. B. Landsdorf. Miss Clara Ledbetter is a sheer intrusion, copied from the writer's notebook. Almost redeemed, but not quite, because the reader still has the sense of a hard plot-line dominance, which is of course the curse of the anecdotal story, and particularly those with a trick or gimmick ending. Characters seem filled in by Central Casting. (D. B. Landsdorf might be played by S. K. Chagall, that adorable ancient dumpling.) Wonderfully warm characters, each doing his bit-part, but nonetheless cast by the author, not organically necessary to the story.

If we had not seen Miss Gordimer's art so beautifully created in some of the stories already discussed, we would allow her a modest bow for these little pieces of French derivation. But, we are spoiled.

IV *Prewar Intellectuals and the French Method*

"Face from Atlantis" is of the French connection in another sense. It is a commentary on the posturing of prewar intellectuals, but in a story made unsteady by the failure to make a vital continuum of conceptual content and the creation of character and incident. Once more, idea emasculates character, creating parodies and stereotypes to demonstrate a point, usually a point best left to the essay form.

"Atlantis" is the pre–World War II world of Waldeck Brand in Heidelberg. As the story opens, we find the Brands on a journey of rediscovery and recapture. In London, by a series of seeming miracles, they meet several of Brand's youthful companions. All seem to have fashioned new lives, adapting to a new language, environment, pace. But one is missing: Carlitta, the intense black-haired, petite beauty—the one most often mentioned by Brand, and by the others, for that matter. Rumor has her somewhere in America.

In New York, the Brands encounter Stefan, a particular friend of Waldeck. Stefan has more particular word: Carlitta had been in New York for some years, living with Klaus, her good Dobbin, whom (as they fully remember) she would never marry. After Klaus removed himself from the scene by going to Mexico, Carlitta lived for a time in Greenwich Village. After that, rumors again—Stefan has heard that she had married a farmer and was living in the Midwest.

Two nights after getting this gem from Stefan, Eileen Brand comes out of the ladies' room to see her husband embracing a small, dark-haired woman. Standing awkwardly nearby is a large, sunburned man. Of course, it is Carlitta and her Ohio husband. In another miracle of coincidence the fabulous flirt from Atlantis has at last been found.

We see her through Eileen's eyes:

Oh, that was the head she had seen before, all right; that was the head that, hair so sleek it looked like a satin turban, inclined with a mixture of coquetry, invitation, amusement and disdain toward a ridiculously long cigarette holder. That hair was brown, after all not the Spanish black of the photographs and imagination. And the face. Well, there is a stage in a woman's life when her face gets too thin or too fat. This face had reached that stage and become too thin. It was a prettily enough shaped face, with a drab, faded skin, as if it was exposed to but no longer took color from the sun. Toward the back of the jaw line, near the ears, the skin sagged sallowly. Under the rather thick, attractive brows the twin caves of the eyes were finely puckered and mauvish. In this faded, fading face (it was like an old painting of which you are conscious that it is being faded away by the very light by which you are enabled to look at it) the eyes had lost nothing; they shone on, greedily and tremendous, just as they had always been, in the snow, reflecting the Neckar, watching the smoke unfurl to the music of the guitar. They were round eyes with scarcely any white to them, like the beautiful eyes of Negro children, and the lashes, lower as well as upper, were black and thick. Their assertion in that face was rather awful.[14]

The unwary reader might well be puzzled at the animus of this cold-eyed catalog of gerontology, so pitiless and even venomous. Nothing in Eileen's character, nor in her response to meeting her husband's old friends, had prepared us for this dry chill.

Astonishment, at first unspoken but soon overt, that the sophisticated Carlitta should marry a chicken farmer from Ohio—named Hicks of all names—continues into the succeeding days; social plans are hindered:

"I don't know what we can do with the husband," said Waldeck, shrugging and giggling.
"That's all right," said Stefan. "Alice will talk to him. Alice can get along with anybody." His wife laughed goodnaturedly.[15]

Alice does, indeed, discover that Edgar Hicks can talk horses, and while the others reminisce with Carlitta about the old days, she occupies him.

But the author, not content with having made a not-very-interesting point with Hicks, is relentless. How had Hicks and Carlitta met? On a train, it is revealed:

"I was sittin' in the diner havin' a beer with my dinner, and in comes this little person looking [what, not "lookin'?] mighty proud and cute as you can make 'em." So it went on, the usual story, and Edgar Hicks spared them no detail of the romantic convention.[16]

Would that Miss Gordimer had spared the reader. Her carica-ture is almost as bad as the American lover in Galsworthy's *The Forsyte Saga*. The satirist, to engage the full attention and respect of the reader for his wit, must be accurate, must be on target. A misplaced snicker is fatal for him, as Hemingway discovered with his unfortunate attempted satire in *A Moveable Feast.*

Carlitta gets defensive when the unspoken question surfaces. What had happened in those four years in the Village to bring her from

the arrogant, beautiful, "advanced" girl with whom Waldeck and Stefan could not fall in love because they and she agreed they were not good enough for her, to the girl who would accept Edgar Hicks a few weeks after a meeting on a train. Carlitta felt the gaze of the girl from South Africa. A small patch of bright color appeared on each of Carlitta's thin cheekbones.[17]

Her tone and manner become more insistent as she elaborates on the virtues of rural Ohio life, the work ethic as well as the sylvan beauties. She concludes with a story of city friends who had dropped in on a working farm day. A storm was coming up; the hay had to come in. So Carlitta put pitchforks in their hands, and despite gauzy frocks and fragile shoes, sent them to work in the fields.

"You should have seen their faces," Carlitta laughed gleefully. "Should have seen their shoes."

The young girl from South Africa felt suddenly angry. Amid the laughter, she said quietly, "I think it was an awful thing to do. If I'd been a guest I should have flatly refused."

"Eileen!" said Waldeck mildly. But Carlitta pointedly excluded from her notice the girl from South Africa.[18]

The lesson in tact and hospitality offered by Eileen goes unnoticed by the laughing men: " 'Just like Carlitta,' " they say. Eileen can't contain herself. She finds herself standing, ready to shout that the old Carlitta in their enchanted memories did not exist anymore; instead was this middle-aged, small, faded woman:

As she opened her mouth to tell them, a strange thing happened. It seemed that her whole mind turned over and showed her the truth. And the truth was much worse than what she had wanted to tell them. For they were right—Carlitta had not changed. They were right, but not in the way they thought. Carlitta had not changed *at all* and that was why there was a sense of horror about meeting her. That was why she was totally unlike any one of the other friends they had met. Under that faded face in that worn body, was the little German girl of the twenties, arrogant in a youth that did not exist, confidently disdainful in the possession of a beauty that was no longer there.[19]

The story closes with a shared laugh at Edgar Hicks. Stefan, in Philadelphia on business, had been charged with looking up Carlitta. He admits that he

"had a hell of a job dodging that Edgar Hicks.... Every time I saw a panama hat with a paisley band I had to double my tracks and go the other way. Once I just managed to squeeze into an elevator in time."

And they all laughed, as if they had just managed it, too.[20]

This curious, unsteady little story—particularly unsteady in management of point of view—almost leads one to the general conclusion that women writers should be licensed for satire, with that license periodically up for review on the point of subjective venom. The overkill done on Carlitta, and especially upon the inoffensive Edgar Hicks, leads one to suspect that personal animus outside the framework of the story is responsible for the distortion. Nothing in the events concerning Mr. and Mrs. Hicks (or in the prewar behavior of Carlitta) justifies the devastation attempted. So, a backlash occurs, damaging to the author's credibility. Or, perhaps the story needs a footnote for the American reader, who is quite accustomed to the myth of rural virtue; who is quite content with seeing James Stewart or Van Johnson take the sophisticated city girl away to fresh milk, sunshine, and clover fields. And she, it is taken for granted, will grow tanned, healthy, and spiritually healed.

The Novels

CHAPTER 5

The Lying Days

NADINE Gordimer's first novel, *The Lying Days*,[1] was published in 1953, a year after her first collection of short stories, *The Soft Voice of the Serpent*. Which means that the novel and the short stories (the finest of her novels and many of her finest stories) were written before the end of her twenties.

The Lying Days takes its title from W. B. Yeats:

> Though leaves are many, the root is one
> Through all the lying days of my youth
> I swayed my leaves and flowers in the sun
> Now I may wither into the truth.

A subtitle might be found in the novel, on page 167. The girl is on a train going home in the heat of summer:

And sitting in the physical reality of the heat that tacked my mind down to consciousness of every part of my body, sweating or touching in discomfort against the encumbrance of cloth, I had an almost physical sensation of being a stranger in what I had always taken unthinkingly as the familiarity of home. I felt myself among strangers; I had grown up, all my life, among strangers: the Africans whose language in my ears had been like the barking of dogs or the cries of birds.[2]

The reader, ruminating upon the events and places in the short stories, particularly those in *The Soft Voice of the Serpent,* will remember the many lives among strangers: the girl on the train, a stranger to her new husband who triumphantly brings back the suddenly strange and unwanted Van Dyke lion; the many sojourner stories (for example "A Bit of Young Life");

the girl on the veld and her violent encounter with the black purse-snatcher ("Is There Nowhere Else Where We Can Meet?"); the young couple at the resort hotel with their new-found friend who catches the great fish. Trains, resort hotels, walks alone in native streets, teeming parties where we stroll as strangers, taking those marvelous quick shots with our candid camera. Even in the family we are strangers; even in bed with a lover we are strangers, taking meticulous, beautiful notes.

So it is with *The Lying Days,* an appealing, impressionistic novel of alienation and search. It is the best of Miss Gordimer's novels because of the vividly done imagery: the mine towns, the sea, the university—all are intensely realized with no more structure than "a child grows up." Her girl does "wither into the truth," through leaving the family home, through love affairs, through exposure to the ferment of university life. But her girl does not, as yet, have the dry harshness, the weary passivity and skepticism which approaches misanthropy, of the later novels, and especially *A Guest of Honour.*

The Lying Days is divided into three books: "The Mine," a short book of childhood and youth in the mine village near Johannesburg; "The Sea," a longer book of young womanhood away from the family, with an important first love; and "The City," also a long book about the university, new friends, stimulating ideas, urban and ethnic problems, and the discovery, like that of Emma Bovary, that lovers can become boring too.

I *"The Mine"*

"The Mine" introduces Helen, nicknamed Nell, a fair red-headed Scots girl. Her parents are to be away for a day, and the girl takes advantage of her freedom for a walk down the street of the mine village:

There were dozens of natives along the path. Some lay on the burned grass, rolled in their blankets, face down, as if they were dead in the sun. Others squatted and stood about shouting, passed on to pause every few yards and shout back something else. Quite often the exchange lasted for half a mile, bellowed across the veld until one was too far away to do more than wave a stick eloquently at the other. A boy in an old dish-cloth walked alone, thrumming a big wooden guitar painted with gilt roses. Orange peels and pith were thrown about, and a persistent fly kept settling on my lip. But I went on rather faster and determined, waving my hand impatiently before my face and watching a white man who stood outside one of the stores with his hands on his hips while a shopboy prized open a big packing case. The Mine boys sauntering and pushing up and down the pavement jostled the man, got in the way. He kept jerking his head back in dismissal, shouting something at them. . . . the air had a thick smell of sweat and strange pigment and herbs, and as I came to the door of the eating house, a crescendo of heavy, sweet nauseating blood-smell, the clamor of entrails stewing richly, assailed me like a sudden startling noise.[3]

We get five pages of the rich putrescence assaulting the girl: the natives with toenails like horn; the rotten smell of oranges; a boy urinating at the curb; smeary shop-windows, chickens underfoot; people like shadows in the dark, redolent interiors. "This is life—this is the real thing!" is her thought, even as her heart runs "fast and trembly." She walks swiftly, holding her buttocks stiffly together.

Then the girl arrives (to make the author's point) at the bland and sterile propriety of the tennis club. "Just in time for tea." The idea behind the juxtaposition is a fruitful one for Miss Gordimer. It appears, in various forms, many times.

A fat, fair man waves back the crumpets. "Do you want to weigh me down and give yourself the advantage?" —They laughed helplessly again; he was the comedian of the crowd, he was always coming out with something. In fact, he had such a reputation for being amusing that they laughed, found their mouths twitching in reflex everytime he opened his, no matter what he said. I laughed with them. Soon I was handing round the crumpets, helping with fresh cups of tea. . . .[4]

The child accepts all varieties of life uncritically, with wide, observant eyes. In book 3, subjected to university teachings, she sorts out her values much more sharply. Question (to be confronted later): what relationship have ideas and values to good writing? But for now, with this gentle satire before us, intensified by juxtaposition with the rich vitality of the native street, we begin to know the girl—what she will love and what she will reject.

In the next chapter we get a closer view of the bourgeois life the girl leads in the white colony of the gold-mining town: her school uniform with the black stockings and the odor of chalk and ink which she brings with her from school; the eau de cologne presence of her mother, and the eternal gossipy women's parties. But the chatter of women's voices ends when father comes home; the afternoon belongs to the ladies; the evenings to the men.

This is home and family. She goes to the store with her mother, and while mother gossips and shops, she prowls the store, making wishes over pretty things. Their lives are timed to the mine whistle in a regular rhythm—except when it howls an emergency. One such occurs on a Sunday, and Mr. Shaw must hasten to the mine; daughter tags along. A huge gathering of native mine workers blots out the green of the manager's yard. The problem has something to do with their mealie-porridge, the way it is prepared. It is soon settled, and afterwards the gathered whites have their tea, with scones.

So goes adolescence, with the first dance, the first corsage, and (with World War II in progress) boys in uniform at the dances.

II *"The Sea"*

Book 2, "The Sea," takes us to the farm, down on the Natal coast, of mother's old friend, Alice Koch. Nell is not seventeen; she has been out of school a year. She arrives in blinding sunlight and heat, solitary at a bleak little station with the sea booming on one side and the lush green jungle of Natal inland. Soon there is damp kiss from the motherly German, Mrs. Koch, and a young man in shorts and an army shirt: Ludi, her son, home on leave. Her first love occurs before the holiday is over.

Mrs. Koch is also fragrant with eau de cologne, but there are no home strictures. Life is easygoing in the openly senti-mental family. Mother and son are very fond of each other,

demonstrably. Nell is warmed and enchanted in the home.
The days are sea-glitter and haze, the evenings are talk,
reminiscence. The girl, innately withdrawn, observant and self-
contained, responds to the ready tears when talk turns to a
happier past. The mother and son, by their intimate sharing
of the small things in household routine, teach the girl something she had not known: a language of love.

Once, in the rain, Nell and Mrs. Koch go to the store, which
"smelled of mice and millet and tobacco," and have tea with
the storekeeper and his wife. A friendly, easy way of life
embraces the girl. The rain stops, and on their way home Ludi
comes to meet them: "A bird called out somewhere as if the
day were beginning over."

The sea is life, fecundity, and beauty; and lying beside it, she
becomes conscious of her own bodily being, warming in the
sun. Her talks with Ludi soon take on a Thoreauvian cast; he
is bitter and scornful of the narrow life of the towns, when
compared to the freedom and naturalness of life by the sea.
Then Ludi, his leave over, must go back to the army. That
afternoon the household subsides into comfortable feminine
tasks. They go for a sedate walk; later fix themselves a rather
meaningless supper.

Suddenly the slam of a car door is heard, and it's Ludi
back. A bridge is out because of the heavy rains last week,
and he cannot make his train. He has wired for an extension
of his leave. Let us lift our heads for a moment to note Miss
Gordimer's feeling for the anticlimax here, even if it must
be brought off by a rather transparent contrivance. Anticlimax
as a token of superior reality has been with us in fiction at
least since Chekhov, certainly with Stephen Crane, and in
full bloom with Hemingway. "'I'm going for a swim,'" says
Ludi. It's dark, but Mrs. Koch says, "'Ludi, why don't you
take Helen?'" Helen hasn't been out all day. A night swim and
the confused excitement of a first kiss follow, with the cold
grittiness of sand and the smell of wet khaki.

Next day, Nell's awkwardness at breakfast is obvious; the
food sticks in her throat. Then Mrs. Koch suggests they all go
to the beach for the day. The girl is resentful (the beach is
their place); but once there she finds a happiness welling up—

family love and family fun restore normal dimensions to her
emotions—and her new, exciting love falls into its place with
this old, welcome love. She lies in the sun, self-consciously
ripening like a fruit. In a secluded cove of the beach, Ludi
kisses her again, more thoroughly. She makes the astonishing
discovery that this love is warmth too, but of a sort she had
not known before.

This enchanted time of first love, written with Miss Gordimer's most dazzling vividness of sense impression: gritty sand,
blinding sun, moist warmth of bodies, booming sea, is fully
up to the finest writing in the short stories. The moments of
the girl's growth are beautifully real; and functionally their
lyric qualities prepare us for the realities of the withering
to come later.

On an afternoon when they have the house to themselves,
they experiment further; but Ludi holds back, sensing how far
Nell is really ready to go, saving her from what he feels would
be self-disgust. Ludi is soon gone, this time for real, to the
army, and Nell lives in a restless dream. Once Mrs. Koch
shows a snapshot of Ludi with a neighbor's young wife—an
unhappy girl, Mrs. Koch sighs—and Ludi had stayed overnight
on a visit once. Ludi had confessed that he had slept with a
girl.

This is the girl, I told the sullen Ludi, not looking at me, not looking
at the sun. And in his refusal to meet the eye of the camera, in the
obstinate stance of his legs—in the silence of that photograph of him—
he confirmed it to the tingling of my half-pain, my curiosity.[5]

II *The University*

Back home "to use the anonymous presence of people" and
thus to retain her secret world with Ludi, Nell does the old
pre-Ludi things—a trip to the town swimming pool, with
giggling girls and coarse grinning boys, but she feels more
than ever her loneliness. At midyear, with Ludi in the Italian
campaign, and with family urging, she decides she must attend
the university in Johannesburg.

University makes her once more the sojourner, the stranger;

first encounters, always awkward, and the enduring sense of alienation:

And so in August I began the first of many hundreds of daily journeys from Atherton to Johannesburg by train. When the line left Atherton station, it ran in the direction of the Mine, and there was a siding just outside the limits of Mine property. Here the train stopped for a minute or two and here I boarded it, every morning, waiting with a handful of other people poised like starters at a race for its screeching arrival, and getting off in the early winter dark in the evening, dropped from day with a soft thud to the dust of the platform. The siding was a bare place of deep red dust and coal grit, where the wind fought torn newspapers and the tin ticket office seemed to be perpetually closed, the man in charge sat so far inside it, and the little bleary window had such a look of ignoring everything, like a closed eyelid.[6]

On the train she meets Joel Aron, a Jewish student who wishes to be an architect. His parents operate a store in the native district, and in fact he has seen Nell with her parents; he remembers her clearly since her childhood, but she has no recollection of him. We, of course, have met him before in the short stories (sometimes a boy, sometimes a girl) in the family-store situations.

Not surprisingly, we meet Joel's family and he meets Nell's before we get into much of the university scene. In Joel's home she finds his mother "with the swollen doll's body from which it seems impossible that tall sons and daughters can, and do, come." In their talk at his home, she is once more the stranger. She sits on the bed while their arguments go over and about her. She observes their Jewish rituals of food and family relationships; she empathizes with Joel's estrangement. In his turn, Joel meets her parents and encounters cliché bigotry. Says her father patronizingly: "That's a well-mannered boy—they know how to bring up their children to respect older people."

Nell soon gets into race disagreements with Joel. Her mother has an Old Black Mammy relationship with Anna, the old native servant; Nell feels that her mother is being condescending. Joel defends her mother's attitude as being more human than Nell's "abstract love of humanity." Then Nell makes the acquaintance of Mary Seswayo, a black student who is virtually a pariah at the university; Joel accuses her of tokenism, in comparison with her mother's fifteen-year friendship with Anna.

A crisis occurs when Nell wishes to bring Mary home for a ten-day study session. Her mother is evasive:

> "Well, I don't know," she said. "I'll have to speak to your father."
> That was what she always said when she did not know whether or not she wanted to do something. I had heard her say it in shops hundreds of times, when she suspected that she might get what she wanted elsewhere, or that she was being overcharged: "I'll have to speak to my husband." Yet I knew that she had never sought my father's advice in her whole life, and he had never cared to have any authority over her or questioned any decision of hers. It was her way of playing for time to go into consultation with herself.[7]

The questions on mother's mind are: " 'Where would she sleep? Where would she eat? Where would she wash?' " Those questions never arose with Anna, for of course she was not in the household on a supposedly equal status.

Mother's answer is " 'No' " and that begins an escalation into a family emotional storm: "My mother climbed slowly and mightily into her anger like a knight putting on his vestments for battle." The gist of mother's aria is that Nell is too good now for her friends; her old schoolmates she has no time for—no, now Helen likes to roll in the mud with her radical friends, like Joel, a Jew brought up among Kaffirs. Mother and daughter become shrill. "You disgust me," cries the girl. It ends with mother bursting into tears and running from the room. "She cried like a man; it had always been hard for her to cry." Nell's leaving home ends book 2.

IV *"The City"*

Part of Nell's estrangement from her family life was the attraction of other life styles among her new university friends: casual clutter, dirty dishes allowed to stand; traditions of etiquette abandoned; and new ideas about the family, about social change. One such household is that of the Marcus family, a careless, touseled, intellectual couple. Jenny gains Nell's enthralled attention when she nurses her baby in mixed company. When she leaves home, Nell goes to live with Jenny and John Marcus in their Japanese-Swedish flat with its charming dishevelment. She is enchanted by their way of life; they live frugally, yet with taste. They seem to be living proof that two people of diverse backgrounds—he Jewish, she Protestant—can create an harmonious and complementary oneness. She shares their lives fully: picnics, relaxed evenings at home, music. She is aware, even, of their lovemaking in the next room.

Then, one day, there appears at the door a dazzling sojourner from Rhodesia: Paul Clark. Paul had been reared on a farm in Natal, spoke two Bantu languages with colloquial ease; had gone from the feudal life of a young plantation squire to the study of law, to the Native Affairs Department. He had just returned from Rhodesia, where he had done research for his Ph.D. His work is that of welfare officer in native locations. Paul is fascinating to Nell; not only his conversation, but his fullness of participation in life, his vitality. And, she admits, there is a "quick blood-attraction of sex on him like the gloss on the plumes of a bird." She feels the return of the delightful warmth in his nearness that Ludi had created; but Paul is all vitality and involvement with people, where Ludi had been remote and self-absorbed.

They all go to a place called Marcel's Cellar, a self-consciously Bohemian gathering-place where the young can sit, drink wine, and escape The Establishment. There are candles in bottles; everyone lounges on mattresses or dances on the rough concrete floor. Nell likes the place: "it was ridiculous, self-conscious, pathetic in its attempt to be dramatically sordid, but it was fun." Nell feels "again the sense of drift, of alienation from the abstractions coming out of people's mouths—my own and others—" and is quietly amused at the scene. That is, until Paul dances with her sensuously; a kind of "midnight frenzy" perfumes the heavy air. Paul kisses her "delicately and passionately" and she leans in voluptuous relief against him, glad to be not thinking:

I smiled to Paul in the dark half-jokingly: "We're just like the rest."
He said, "Of course."[8]

Nell discovers that she is "a giver," and she becomes excited
by the "desire to stake my whole life, gather up from my self
everything I had stored against such a moment, and expend it
all on Paul."

V *Living with Paul*

They make love and begin a prolonged affair, the next Sunday
afternoon. The affair is described after the sexual fact; she is
concerned with sexual etiquette, characteristically, and wishes
to verbalize events, afraid that, in her inexperience, she had not
been adequate. Nell goes to live with Paul, as Jenny and John
Marcus break up their flat. She had kept in touch with her family,
and they approve of Paul as a proper prospect for marriage—
not knowing, of course, that she is living with him.

She is sustained by the important feeling that Paul, a social
worker for the natives, is at grips with the most vital social problem in the nation. The Nationalists, with Malan, are in power;
the flow of laws leading to *apartheid* has begun. There is a ban
on mixed marriages; the newspapers tell of devoted couples after
years of marriage, parted in official decrees of shame and disgust.
Paul's daily duties bring him into such affairs. For Nell, because
of this, their affair has the passionate excitement of a wartime
marriage. It becomes a secular personal religion, with its own
fervor and ardency.

She makes a dutiful visit to her parents, just returned from six
months in Europe. She sees her father and mother very nearly
as a vaudeville act, feeding each other straight lines about their
experiences, unwrapping ugly tourist-trap souvenirs of the trip.
Abruptly, Nell tells her mother that she is living with Paul and
gets the expected tongue-lashing, beginning " '—girl from a
decent home—' " and culminating in, " 'I don't want you in this
house again.' " Then her father comes in, and the whole scene
must be played again. But finally it is over, and the three are
able to have an odd tea together:

We even had tea before my father took me to the station. In
silence as if someone had died. While we were sitting at the dining-

room table drinking, the smell of the room when I bent over the table painting from my color box as a child came to me, immediate, complete, unaltered. The print-smell of the pile of English newspapers, the oil-smell of furniture polish, the cool dark fruit-smell from the dish on the sideboard; and the smell of ourselves, us three people, my father, my mother and me, with which everything in the house was impregnated like objects in a sandalwood box, and that, when I took out something from home in the atmosphere of the flat or of the Marcuses' house, gave me the queer feeling of momentarily being aware of myself as a stranger.[9]

In time, like Emma Bovary, she tires of the affair which becomes so much like a stale marriage with its domestic routines of meals and bed-making. She smiles in recollection of her mother's lurid images of "living with a man." One day she meets Joel on the street, and she is reminded of forgotten virginity and innocence, and of being a daughter in a family.

Her only stimulant is societal. There is excited talk of throwing the Nats out; but Paul is troubled by a black separatist movement. Antiwhite sentiment grows among the very people Paul had been working with. Even liberal whites are being excluded from black groups. Sipho, one of Paul's most effective black leaders, and a valuable liaison man, becomes estranged. Paul, after strenuous bureaucratic wangling, has arranged for a sports field. Sipho and his followers decide to boycott it: " 'We don't want kindness; we must have freedom.' " Paul is also immersed in the tremendous problem of the housing shortage; there are twenty times more people than there are houses.

In their intimate lives, coincidentally, their bed becomes overpopulated with two sweating, straining bodies. Their bodies become tyrants; physical compulsion traps them. As Paul's work becomes exasperatingly more difficult, their relationship becomes more difficult.

They begin to see their friends again. We get party-going snapshots once more, with Miss Gordimer's superb camera work: " 'And this is her Paul—' as Isa moves off, not waiting to see where her arrow falls." Once more the alienated, quiet observer:

Depression came over me and drew me back from the other people in the room, so that being incapable of being involved with any of them, I seemed to see all the several groups at once, to watch their mouths shaping talk and their faces and bodies supplementing and contradicting what they said. I felt a dull envy for Isa, taking the small pleasure of triumphs of her tongue. I thought almost with longing of the struggles she must have given up to content herself with the substitute of these things; and I wished for a moment that I were clever enough to be able to ignore their unreality and emptiness, or that I was another kind of person, a person for whom they could ever have some meaning. In that room full of people whom I knew well enough to fear their curiosity, I wanted to cry. In a bus, in a train, among strangers I would have cried, as people sometimes have to, cannot always wait to be alone. But here I dared not, and so all these people my friends, became enemies.[10]

Like Emma, Helen at this stage must find her meaning for life in a variety of romantic apocalypse; when that pales, she is lost. She and Paul begin to quarrel seriously. Nell quits her job at the African welfare agency, and it becomes recognized mutually that they will never marry. At this crucial time, her father calls to find out how she is. His shy concern reaches her; she decides she must go home.

Home is a return to reclusive childhood: the store, the tea, the gossip of the Mine, Sunday afternoons on the lawn. No mention is made of her affair; it's as if she had been ill, and needs quiet for convalescence. Mine talk recalls that time years ago when the trouble at the mine had been over tea serving. " 'Ah, but things were done decently in those days,' " says one of the mine officers. Not like the one coming up on Monday. The one coming up Monday is to be the explosive May Day strike, in which Nell is to find herself involved, see a man killed, and be caught in a maelstrom of rioting and violence.

At dusk, on Monday, she goes in search of Paul at the community center. She is suddenly in the midst of a wall of shouting natives; stones are thrown, glass is broken. Before the night is over, eighteen natives are dead; one of them is Sipho, the native leader Paul had worked so well with.

Then comes apathy and indolence for a month, until her shock heals itself. Then it comes to her, quite simply, that she wants to go away, to Europe. Soon Helen is off on a journey of convalescence—ship, airline, hotel—finding an oasis in the trivial rituals of travel: meals, deck chairs, viewing. The detail is vivid by habit, but irrelevant in function except for delineating a bored self-awareness.

She meets Joel, and they spend an afternoon of fine inconsequence. He has found a purpose: to go off to Israel to a new life. Their conversation is of chances missed—to know each other, to become involved. The fault is in withholding the self, perhaps because he's Jewish, she Gentile. Joel confesses his love, and she weeps. Parting from him is more poignant than leave-taking from Paul. She is leaving youth and idealism, and devoted, uncomplicated love. Joel represents these elements in her own nature, hence to say good-bye to him is to say good-bye to her own innocent youth. It is interesting that in this first book, more autobiographical than any of the succeeding novels, Miss Gordimer assumes the persona of a red-haired, fair-skinned girl of Scottish descent, projecting her own ambivalent Jewish persona into the character of Joel.

The next day after leaving Joel, she begins to feel that failure can sometimes be a blessing; that disillusionment and sadness can be the beginnings of a new life. As she thinks these things, she hears native children singing in the morning air outside her window, and the novel closes upon this image of promise and hope.

CHAPTER 6

A World of Strangers

I N the short stories, particularly the ones that fail to come off
well, and in some of the social conflict portions of *The Lying
Days*, we have seen Miss Gordimer becalmed in the arid wastes
of sociology. Her situations are derived from essay posturings,
and her conversations become polemical declarations by caricatures rather than the beautifully realized characters she is
capable of creating.

Her second novel, *A World of Strangers*,[1] unfortunately takes
for its milieu the very arena of social change which has been her
bête noir in the short fiction: urban society, the vanity fair of
pseudoliberals in their eternal parties; the white slumming in
African locations, or displaying token Africans daringly; and
finally, direct racial encounters.

A further unfortunate circumstance in the novel is the choice
of a protagonist: a young man from England, who has come to
South Africa to seek his fortune with a publishing house. He
is a thinly disguised instrument, quite closely akin to Miss
Gordimer's alienated but perceptive young woman. Even without
that handicap of ambivalence, he suffers from having no compelling story to engage our attention; he is a rather neutral
observer in the affairs of South Africa, a Boswell without a
Dr. Johnson. In her most recent novel, *A Guest of Honour*, which
is also told from the point of view of a male protagonist, Miss
Gordimer manages the narration much more interestingly; not
only does the narrator evince a more believable maleness but
he has a much more functional role in the events of the story.
In *A World of Strangers*, however, the protagonist never holds
us. Despite the vivid realization of place, the quick and vivid
snapshots which tell us that we are reading Nadine Gordimer,
there is no immersion in a life, or a love, to compel our con-
tinued page-turning.

106

As a novel it must rank far below *The Lying Days*; but its failures are interesting ones, both for an understanding of Miss Gordimer's art (the study of failure is often more useful to the critic than the study of success) and for an understanding of the pitfalls lying in wait for the novelist of African social history.

A World of Strangers is a short novel with a prologue and five parts. There is a motto from the writings of Federico Lorca:

> I want the strong air of the most profound night
> to remove flowers and letters from the arch where you sleep
> and a black boy to announce to the gold-minded whites
> the arrival of the reign of the ear of corn.[2]

The lines are favorites of Miss Gordimer (they appear also in *The Lying Days*). The application to this novel is that possibly they forecast for the "gold-minded whites" of South Africa the coming ascendency of the native blacks and their "reign of the ear of corn." That last would indicate the naturalness, perhaps even the nobility of natives. One should note parenthetically that the staple diet of tribal natives in South Africa is "mealies," a dish that Americans would recognize as cornmeal mush; perhaps Miss Gordimer was amused by the Lorca image as applied to the aspirations of South African blacks.

The short prologue of the novel offers a familiar Nadine Gordimer situation—sojourners, this time aboard the ship bringing young Mr. Hood to Africa. The people, some tourists, some returning to their homeland, are targets for quick, candid shots. The commentary is acrid and metallic as we come to know the Turgells—the mother and the daughter Rina ("'What an odd, patronizing child she is—'"). The mother becomes ill at the thought of putting foot on African soil again, and Hood thinks, "Were these the sort of people Africa gets? Christ, poor continent!"[3]

Hood had grown up in a home where imperialism was deplored; where the grandfather who was killed at Jagersfontein and had been cited for bravery was not honored: "'Like celebrating Franco's victory in Spain,'" his mother had said. His position with a publishing firm, and some family connections, give him an entrée into the business world as well as the art and

theatrical circles of Johannesburg. He is taken up by Hamish
Alexander and introduced to the Wanderer's Club set, which is
to furnish Toby with much of material for his satiric and rejective
bent. Alexander is a board-of-directors sort "with the perpetual
smile of a man who has many guests." Toby, by contrast, has a
quiet gift for snobbery, of which we get a sample upon his
first visit to the office:

> Miss McCann, who was one of those common little girls to whom
> anaemia gives a quenched look which may be mistaken for refinement,
> and who, appropriately, smelled of sickroom cologne. I should have
> to find some means of getting rid of her.[4]

He does "get rid" of her before long, after his immersion in
the vitality of the black society of Johannesburg.

At the Hamish Alexanders, he hears talk of sports, of safaris,
of horses; meets "good looking women who smelled luxurious,"
one of whom is Cecil Rowe, a sophisticate who takes a fancy to
him. In due time, he will have a rather lackluster affair with her;
its purpose in the novel is apparently as counterpoint to the more
meaningful life of the black community.

Quick party shots give us a kaleidoscope of a series of
caricatures:

> —the kind of couple whose clothes—in this instance riding clothes—
> might have been donated by some firm in return for having them
> worn to advantage, and in the right company.[5]

Or this: "The two latest were youthfully apoplectic, blond, with
small, flat, lobeless ears, short noses, and bloodshot blue eyes."[6]
With these two latest guests is an American girl with a long
cigarette holder who "flickered a kind of lizard-look over everyone." Later on, finding herself nearby Toby, she turned her head
toward him

> and said, in a low, dead American voice, "I hear you're a gread wrider."
> "No, no, just a publisher," I said, embarrassed because I wasn't
> really even that, yet. At which she burst out laughing—a bold, full
> laugh, surprisingly in contrast to her speaking voice—and said: "I
> guess I've got the wrong purson."[7]

None of these people, with the exception of Cecil, is to figure greatly in the future of Toby; they are tone-setters, conditioning the reader to turn with relief to the naturalness and vitality of the black community.

Toby finds a flat, moves in, attends other parties just as deadly, and settles into his duties. His encounters with the African community begin with a visit from Anna Louw, a Legal Aid lawyer. She has come to him because of a bureaucratic snarl involving a black member of his staff. The mother of Amon Mofeking is being evicted from her freehold home in one of the removals to new locations for native blacks; in the new housing, the blacks get no freeholds. Amon must have the day off to help Anna fight the case. Anna, a "short, dark woman with the neat head of a tidy woman" is a staunch advocate for the rights of the natives. Her visit to Toby's office leads to the offer of a ride; finally to Toby's first multiracial party. This party is different from those of the Wanderer set. Africans, Indians, and liberal whites all gathered voluntarily, with their faces alight, talking animatedly, and laughing, offer a quite new experience for Toby.

A black man initiates conversation with Toby, in itself remarkable for him. The man is Steven Sitole, destined to play a major part in Toby's African experience. The talk is of Tolstoy, of serious art, of racial politics. The wine and the food are relished. Then Steven and a girl named Dorothea dance, like professionals. Toby dances with Anna, who does not drink: "She had the air of distinctness that a sober person has in a room where everyone else's aura is quickened and blurred by euphoria—as if their souls were in motion while hers was still. 'Good party,' Toby said."[8] A black girl, who has been sitting quietly by the wall, stands and begins singing: "All the warm, continuous gamut of sensuality was there, from the mother's breast to the lover's bed. Delight was like a sudden, simple happiness in the room."[9]

Steven Sitole, who has the compelling magnetism of a black Dick Diver, takes us to a shabby part of town, and a black shebeen (a native speakeasy):

Steven went along with the happy ease of a man who could have found his way in his sleep; he was at home in a dark and lonely street. He sang softly, under his breath, in his own language; so softly, he might have been breathing music.[10]

The reader will have noticed that when observing the natives we drop the satiric candid shots, the cattiness, and the detachment; on the contrary, we are entirely empathic to the people and their conversation. In the shebeen we talk Dostoevski, philosophy, and the politics of race. In the midst of the good talk and the warm human feeling, we have to hustle out a window—police raid. The evening ends in a harum-scarum chase through back alleys of the district Steven knows so well, and finally: "We lay there panting and laughing in swaggering, schoolboy triumph."

Toby's relationship to Steven throughout the book is a puzzling one. There is a complete, passive followership to Toby's manner and behavior; and he has a sensual awareness of Steven's ears, his eyes, his body, that to the Freudian critic would be unmistakable: an unrecognized homosexuality.

I would defend Miss Gordimer from that putative appraisal on several grounds: first, she has demonstrated in many stories and novels a full awareness of sexual relationships. She can be quite overt when it suits her purpose; or she can be subtle if it pleases her. If she had wished to imply a homosexual relationship here, she would have done so with complete control of all nuances. Secondly, Miss Gordimer is interested in other game than the sexual. The interplay of personality, the capacity for love in the sense of *caritas,* the meaning of death, especially death in life—all of these exist in the troubled arena of South African society. Miss Gordimer, in short, is the inheritor of the Chekhov, Joyce, Mansfield tradition, and could not be satisfied with pigeonholing her characters with Freudian labels. Thirdly, in essays and lectures she has scoffed at the too simplistic assumptions of sexual motivation, particularly as they occur in racial situations.

This is not to say that she is entirely successful in her management of the Toby-Steven relationship; it is a puzzling and confusing one, but one which I put down to a technical unsteadiness. This is Miss Gordimer's first try, in the novel form, at a male protagonist. At times he is given a wholly feminine sensitivity, as for instance early in part 2 of the novel. Toby has called Steven and asked him to lunch, at Toby's flat. He buys food, sets out the wine, puts the place to rights, and prepares for his guest. Steven doesn't come. Toby waits several hours. Finally he sits down and eats alone, disappointed and rather forlorn. The stand-up, and Toby's response to it, present a feminine situation and a feminine hurt: the presumed rejection by someone fondly anticipated, someone who has promised to come to you, and, without explanation, does not come.

The texture of man-to-man life escapes Miss Gordimer on occasions in the novel. Later on, Toby meets Steven at Anna's. They talk about Toby's need for a car:

Anna asked me how I got there. And then we got talking about the car I needed, and what kind it should be, and where I should get it. The subject of cars is paraffin on the fire of talk among most men, and Steven and Sam lighted up at once in passionate discussion.[11]

Why that last sentence? A woman explaining men and cars to other women? The texture of commentary is feminine. Even if the purpose is to show that blacks are just "ordinary folks" who have interests much like whites, the incident is unsteady; in one or two of her short stories, Miss Gordimer satirizes that sort of condescension.

We are soon after at another mixed party, with Steven at the center playing host and making sorties of hospitality. Music starts:

feet moved, heads swayed, there was no audience, no performers— everyone breathed music as they breathed air—. It was a fulfillment, a passion of jazz. Here they danced for joy.[12]

Compared to the arid, snobbish, and vulgar parties of the Wanderer set, this is wholeness, naturalness, life. Except that it is the reader who now stands off, eyebrow lifted, at this transparent aesthetic agitprop. Readers of the proletarian novel, from Zola's *Germinal*, with its similar juxtaposition of the lives of miners and managers, and similar pointed creation of scenes of decadent sterility versus scenes of natural vitality, to the more recent *Grapes of Wrath*, will recognize the feeling.

From the party we go with Steven "into the townships, the shebeens, the rooms and houses of his friends." He is accepted

warmly wherever they go, and Toby, watching with admiration
from a step behind, sees his charm at work. He mimics the
whites, comes out with the latest slang, knows everyone, dances
and laughs through the slums of Sophiatown:

he grinned at me with that careless aplomb, shrugging his shoulders
and looking down his nose at himself, that gave him such an air and
always, wherever we went in the townships, drew the young bloods
about him to hear what he would say next.[13]

Following this stimulating tour of Johannesburg black life,
we go to see Cecil Rowe. It is a dull Sunday morning; the priest
in the Anglican service "advocated Christ as if he were suggesting a course of vitamin pills; the congregation listened
politely."[14]

After church, we surprise Cecil Rowe in bare feet and without makeup. Her curtains are limp and a bouquet of flowers
is dead in a vase. It is "a room of many attempts, all of which
had petered out." Toby goes with her out to the Hamish Alexanders, and has a trivial, boring weekend, riding, swimming,
and partying.

Back in the office on Monday, he has another revealing race-
attitude encounter, this time with Miss McCann (the anemic
girl). He sends out for sandwiches and shares them with Steven
and an Indian friend in his office. An awkwardness results,
which ends with her giving notice, eventually. For that final
occasion, she appears with a stocky, resentful young man—the
resentment is directed at Toby, but it is stifled. Miss McCann
says her piece and goes out:

the young man trooping behind her, like a bull that has been led
into the ring and out again, without using the blind urges in his
breast—all so stupid and petty. A nobody of a girl thinks she's too
good to come into a room where a white man is sharing lunch with
two black men.[15]

Stupid is the right word. This event, and this commentary by
Toby—which supposedly is to have our sympathy—might be
taken as a synecdoche for much of the novel. It is a cheap shot
at cardboard characters to belabor an obvious point—so gross,

so clumsy that the reader lifts his head to ask, "Is this the author of 'The Catch,' 'The Train From Rhodesia,' 'Is There Nowhere Else Where We Can Meet?'" Anger at racial bigotry does indeed jar a fine instrument out of tune. Or, perhaps the lesson here is that the novel form, with its greater demands upon sustained continuity, entices the author into hard confrontations, dramatic scenes, and away from the subtly tangential situations which are her best mode.

A few days later, Toby finds himself rather unenthusiastically in a love affair with Cecil. It begins in a suitably clichéd situation involving exploration of a deserted house. With this movie-set conditioning, Toby kisses Cecil in a way that she interprets instantly. "'Not here,'" she says at once. "Social caution, her only and familiar arbiter, restored her to her known world."[16] One night after dinner, they make love in her living room. There is a complete lack of spontaneity: she is in complete control of her sexual responses; he is aware of the chemical smell of her hair and cosmetics.

Back to life in the native area:

The life in the townships, at such moments, seemed to feed a side of my nature that had been starved; it did for me what Italy and Greece had done for other Englishmen, in other times. It did not change me; it released me and made me more myself.[17]

And he knows well that if he were to tell Cecil that his closest friends were black men, that he ate with them, slept in their houses, she would discard him in disgust and loathing. Instead, we find the affair fading from ennui.

We go to another sort of party where mixed blacks and whites are found. It is a pseudosophisticated group from the theater and the arts; with them, it is a current fad to have a "pet African" who can hold forth in the smart talk of drama or literature. Toby once more feels that he is in a world of strangers. Searching once more for the genuine, he goes to see Anna, to talk with her about her concern for African justice; her whole being is engaged in the strenuous struggle. Before long, almost as "an extension of the conversation," he is engaged in a love affair with her.

Anna is a disillusioned ex-communist. She had made a trip to Russia in 1950, but unlike the ex-communists Toby had known in London, she had not remained in their chronic state of exhaustion, which prevented any new commitment. Instead, she had come back to Africa, where she had been born; not back to the small village in the Karoo, but to Johannesburg, where she operated as a kind of urban frontiersman. Also in her past is a failed marriage with an Indian, Hassim Bhayat. It had failed because the "mixed" quality permeated all relationships, despite their mutual awareness of that possibility. Even their quarrels could not be the normal quarrels between lovers—they became always morbid with race—they used race, as if it could furnish the supreme hurt. Only when race was hurled between them could they feel the quarrel finished; and at last, the marriage ended.

Toby goes to the Hamish Alexanders for a Christmas house party, and then to a black party following soon after—this latter with Sam Mofokenzazi and some of Steven's other friends. Toby takes Sam home and is scolded by the white caretaker of his flat for "natives in the building."

The penultimate book of the novel takes us into the bush-veld with the Hamish Alexanders for a hunting party. The scenery is beautifully captured: the thorn bushes, the kopjies, the wide sky. As in Flaubert, nature imagery counterpoints the stupidity and vulgarity of the human elements. Here the hunters with their vicious mores and their bullying treatment of the natives, are the targets for Miss Gordimer's scorn. Toby is a good shot, thanks to training back in England, and is able to put the hunters down even at their own game.

The final book of the novel is dominated by the death of Steven Sitole. It is a native death, drawn in the pattern of "Six Feet of the Country." The first reports are matter-of-fact police callousness about a stolen coat, which they report having found on a native, one Steven Sitole. He had been in a car with other natives; his identity and the true facts are lost in fumbling and red tape. Sam says, " 'Do you think if he'd been a white man that's all there'd have been for him?' "

After Steven's death, Toby drops his white friends, those met at the Hamish Alexanders; and he sees Cecil only once more. While a woman's voice at the next table provides an irritating, nagging obbligato, Cecil tells of her plans to marry again—to a Johannesburg friend, older and well-to-do.

As he is leaving Johannesburg, he sees a notice in the paper that Anna has been arrested and is to be tried for treason, one of the large number destined to become the *cause célèbre* of the late fifties in South Africa. " 'I'll be back,' " he assures Sam. But Sam says, " 'Who knows, with you people?' " And so, the final rapport, deepened by the sadness of Steven's death, rips apart once more upon the issue of race.

At the station, as he is clipping from the newspaper the notice of Anna's arrest on the treason charge, he sees, on a page that has fallen, the face of Cecil in the social column. She is laughing, and she is with Patterson, the well-to-do man she is to marry. "So I cut that out, too. The two pieces of newspaper rested in my wallet in polarity."[18] With this final polarity of the rich Philistines and the black proletarians, the book ends.

CHAPTER 7

Occasion for Loving

OCCASION for Loving[1] is on all counts a better novel than *A World of Strangers*. The management of viewpoint is more skilled, the patterns of developing relationships offer both more variety and more depth; most of all, Miss Gordimer in this novel has followed the procedure of her best short stories, namely, to immerse the ever-present danger of racial melodrama in other, more complex human situations. The racial materials, in short, are not the first business of the author, but come in tangentially upon other well-established life forms, as they do in such excellent short stories as "The Train from Rhodesia" and "Six Feet of the Country." None of the novels, however, approaches the mastery of the best short stories in this most difficult aspect of technique, and *Occasion for Loving*, while an advance over the prior novel, is no exception.

Jessie Stilwell, the viewing character, is infinitely more interesting, and more useful to the author, than Toby of *A World of Strangers*. Consider for a moment only the most accessible elements of her situation: she is married to Tom Stilwell, each "keeping private harbors." She had been in an early, brief marriage, the product of which was Morgan, a withdrawn, very private boy of fifteen, whose sense of privacy is in some ways a reflection of her own desire. She has three little girls by Tom Stilwell. Morgan, because of his temperament, is present in her marriage with Tom like a chronic house guest—always there, but never really one of the family. This situation is not of Tom's making, quite the contrary, but is a consequence of her own and Morgan's natures.

Jessie's mother is still very largely part of her emotional apparatus. Her own father had died when she was eighteen months old, and when she was age three, her mother married

116

again, an engineer named Bruno Fuecht. The stepfather was such an intrusion into the girl's relationship with her mother—a relationship that she was later to perceive as manipulative and obsessive on her mother's part—that she loathed him. Once, in her teens, she was awakened at night by bathroom noises, and confronted her mother in the hallway. When she questioned her, vaguely sensing outrage, her mother said intensely:

"*Nothing.* Go back to bed." Her mother gave in and appealed to her as a woman.

Bruno Fuecht. He had no name. A creature lying on the other side of a door, in bed as in a lair, love. Her mother, Bruno Fuecht, and—. A conclusion reached only once, in the middle of the night. Left unfinished, forever, in her daytime self. Love. Mrs. Fuecht is so close to her daughter. "My daughter is my life."

At last, she slept beside Tom Stilwell.[2]

She now speaks of her mother as Mrs. Fuecht. A letter comes, telling that Mr. Fuecht has been put into a nursing home. " 'What a queer woman she is,' " she remarks to Tom. " 'She writes with a real air of triumph about it.' "

There are three loves in the web about Jessie: Jessie and her mother, with the second husband that causes Jessie to call her mother Mrs. Fuecht. It remains in her life like an oak gall; she has grown past it, but it distorts in ways she is yet to discover. A second love is her own marriage with Tom, the Dobbin in her life; far more interesting is her enigmatic love for Morgan, often little more than an obligation, a reluctant ritual of affection. The third love is that which acts as catalyst for the major action of the novel, the love which comes into her life shortly after the arrival of Ann and Boaz Davis. Ann is to have an extended affair with a black—a charming painter and teacher, Gideon Shibalo—an event that comes upon Jessie with the blunt economy of synopsis.

Henry James would have liked this design, so far. He would be amused by the motif of manipulation in the mother, although he would have insisted that it be pursued. He would have been delighted by the relationship of Jessie and Morgan, and would have found ways to make it function as a major story relationship rather than the situation image it is here. The desire of

Jessie to be the detached observer, but pushed to the extreme of voyeurism, would have pleased him, and he would have stated it with his genteel sophistication. The functional imagery of garden and home to make clear Jessie's solipsistic yearnings would have appealed to him. He would have liked the idea of an intrusion as catalyst. There we must abandon him, however, for reasons that should emerge as we peruse the novel.

Book 1 of the novel establishes these relationships in a stage-setting sequence of images and events. The novel has two mottoes: one by Boris Pasternak, which gives the book its title: "We have all become people according to the measure in which we have loved people and have had occasion for loving." The other is from Thomas Mann: "In our time the destiny of man presents its meaning in political terms."

The opening paragraph gives us home, garden, and memories of mother; alienation, arid rejection, the mother's oppressive greed for the life of her daughter—all of these are beautifully interwoven:

> Jessie Stilwell had purposefully lost her way home, but sometimes she found herself there, innocent of the fact that she had taken to her heels long ago and was still running. Still running, and the breathlessness and drumming of her feet created an illusion of silence and motionlessness—the stillness we can feel while the earth turns—in which she had never left her mother's house. It happened now, while she walked slackly from out of the shade of the verandah into the hot wind of September that battered and mis-shaped the garden. It blew her dress in behind her knees; she was alone and did not trouble to straighten her back. The tap turned in her palm with a dry squeak; the spray from the hose sounded like a shower of gravel on the parched leaves.... "What's the water-bill going to be this month, I'd like to know!" her mother accused the plants. Nothing grew well in the baked red surface that was given a lick of water once a week. A few coarse, bright blooms—a single iris, a yellow daisy—stuck up like hat-pins.[3]

In her own house, in the present, she resists calling out to Tom: "She hated to make the house restless in the few pauses of peace that fell upon it."

Despite the number of people in the house (the Stilwells' three young girls—the youngest scarcely out of diapers; Morgan, the fifteen-year-old house-guest from the first marriage; a servant; and, of course, Tom and Jessie) Miss Gordimer creates a sense of solitude. Jessie resists involvement with her children; when she is upstairs in her room a quarrel breaks out below—children's shrill contentions, then heavy, purposeful footsteps coming up the stairs. She pushes the door shut: "The heavy breathing outside the door went away. Jessie experienced a moment of what she thought of to herself as childish triumph—she had escaped the child."[4] One might put this down to the very common feeling of any parent, overwhelmed by incessant collisions of bodies and voices and demands in the house. Yet the detachment, the withdrawn self, persists throughout the novel. For example, here is another such moment:

The child kissed her cheek, and then flung her arms around her mother's neck and embraced her passionately. She stood again, her eyes on a level with her mother's; and meeting the child's eyes, Jessie saw them fixed on her, blurred, impassioned, sick with love that would fasten on and suck the life out of her.[5]

With the young Ann and Boaz Davis in the house, Jessie feels the presence of two observers in her life. The reader feels impelled to amend: two *more* detached observers. When she takes Ann Davis up to her room, ordinarily Morgan's:

"I've got rid of all traces of Morgan in here," Jessie said, and added, for truthfulness, "There wasn't much, anyway." She had been surprised to find how little of her son there was in the room; how tenuous his hold on this house was.[6]

Throughout book 1 of the novel, Miss Gordimer has been giving us a very particularized portrait of Jessie Stilwell, with emphasis upon her stifled capacity for loving. Before going on to the present business of living, with its peculiar demands to be made upon that starved capacity—demands related to the race problem in South Africa—we get other cutback events which contribute to the scar tissue formed by the encounter with mother in the hallway, as she steels herself to the sexual serfdom of wifehood.

One is a Christmas weekend in a wretched resort hotel.

Jessie is seventeen, but because of the holiday she must share a bedroom with Mr. and Mrs. Fuecht. It has rained for the whole time of the holiday; the porridge has weevils; there is nothing to do but sit in the shabby lobby and watch the women knitting.

The weekend itself had changed its meaning for Jessie many times before it passed into that harmless state known as forgotten. Just after her young husband died, when she became aware that a large part of her life was missing, that she had been handed from mother to husband to being a mother herself without ever having had the freedom that does not belong to any other time of life but extreme youth—just then, knowing herself cheated, that Christmas weekend had come back to her with revulsion and resentment. There, in that cheap, ugly place, her youth had been finally bound and thrown out into the mud to die, while the middle-aged sat in their chairs.[7]

II *An Emotionally Crippled Woman and her Son*

With this partial case history of an emotionally crippled woman before us, we are ready to take on present events. One event is a rather meaningless trip to see the native dancers at a mine (one of the tourist routines in Johannesburg is a Sunday visit to one of the large gold mines, where native workers do a vaudeville representation of tribal dances). It serves for nothing in the novel, save local color, perhaps; and to give us another shot at Jessie going dutifully through another empty ritual. The phoniness of the dances perhaps does serve as an image of the many empty rituals in Jessie's life: wife, mother, daughter, hostess—and, finally, vicarious lover. She, in a way like the dancers, does a burlesque of activities that should be functional and vitalistic.

Another significant event in book 1 involves Morgan's escapade—he is picked up in a dubious taxi-dance joint in Hillbrow, a Johannesburg suburb. Jessie begins to laugh at the consternation on Tom's face, and at the improbability of the adventure. *Morgan,* of all people! When he comes home late at night, they decide the best procedure is to treat the boy "as if nothing had happened." And, at breakfast, Morgan puts on a good show of unconcern. The boy, "who had always been on the periphery of the life of the house, found himself at the center."[8] Eyes are covertly upon him, but his odd relationship does not change:

There was nothing unnatural about his behavior because he was never natural, but seemed always to be behaving in a way that he timidly and clumsily thought was appropriate.[9]

Morgan's pathetic being is captured in one of Miss Gordimer's beautiful *traits de lumière*:

His presence went unnoticed, though he always kept his face mobile like the face of one of those actors in a crowd scene who, you are surprised to see if you happen to glance at them, have gone on acting all the time the audience has been entirely taken up with the principals. He would never have dared to retire into himself, in company.[10]

Jessie does go to the taxi-dance joint, curious as to why Morgan had been attracted to it. She sits at a table in the cellar ("she thought, with the criticism of one generation for another, how what she had sought had usually to be found in cellars") pretending that she waits for a companion, and observes the bored dancers. One of the men stops at her table. " 'You wouldn't like to dance, madam?' "

The fastidious politeness, the obsequious male pride in knowing how a woman likes to think she's being treated lay in a pathetic gloss over the raven ferociousness of the creature. His mean eyes had an objective loneliness, like the eyes of an animal that does not know it was born behind bars.
She did not learn why Morgan had gone there. To do so, she understood at last, you would first have to know where he set out from.[11]

The reader begins, however, to see a design in these "occasions for loving." The mechanistic rituals of the taxi-dance girls and their pimps were vulgar versions of her own rituals of love, mechanistic in their turn. That Morgan sought out the place is fully understandable. In a way that Jessie could not see, he was simply going home.
Henry James, who comes to mind often in the reading of

this novel, also loved the vulgar "reflector" situation. His structuring of such tarnished mirror images occurs as early as *The American* in which the little copyist, Noemi and her father-pimp are a burlesque overture to the more complex love search involving Claire and her aristocratic family. Insight with the overtones of comic irony result from such an angle-shot.

III *Another "Occasion for Loving"*

A third event in book 1, all in preparation for the major concern of the novel, is the abrupt appearance of Bruno Fuecht. This also turns out to be an "occasion for loving." Presumably in a nursing home, he has taken flight and is on his way to Switzerland. He has liquidated all his holdings, or so he says, partly to spite Mrs. Fuecht but also to finance his new life, his new loves. Tom goes to his hotel "like a paid mourner at a funeral" to see the old man. Jessie has refused.

> He was ill, of course. But it wasn't that. It wasn't just the old men's symptoms of the collar grown too big, the hollow, delicate-looking as the skin over an infant's fontanelle, in front of each blood-less ear. He was blazing behind his line of tight mouth, behind his dark eyes made dominating in the diminished face, by his magnifying glasses; he was blazing like the chandelier.[12]

He blazes with his new lust for life, a last feverish flame. Tom apologizes for the absence of Jessie; Bruno responds:

> "I didn't expect her to come. She's never been much like a daughter. Well, that's an old story. Never mind."
> Tom smiled. "Well, she's only a stepdaughter."
> "Yes, her mother kept that up. For the memory of poor Charles, she said. We both loved poor Charles. Only she couldn't have loved him so much, could she? Eh?"[13]

Tom is bewildered by the words, the surly self-contempt in the old man's voice, the wry guile. Is Jessie really Bruno's daughter by an adulterous affair with Bruno before the idolized "young father" died? Back home, looking at Jessie with these words in mind, Tom is sure that she *knows* she is Bruno's

daughter; hence the venom toward him. But he is also sure
that he will never bring the question up.

The old man's vivid, grotesque appearance, and disappear-
ance (he is soon dead in Rome) is mindful of some of the
minor characters in Joseph Conrad. Conrad had the knack of
giving overwhelming reality to brief, often grotesque appearances, such as the old man in *Lord Jim* in the fly-blown cuddy,
the "last shrine" of Brierly's memory. Conrad's purpose was
not merely to illuminate the scene, but to bring to life some
facet of Jim's heroic dream. Brierly, the official hero, comes to
this shabby end, an ironic comment upon illusory ideals. One
can only speculate upon Miss Gordimer's intention with Mr.
Fuecht. The old literary stratagem of birth error, here hinted
at in Jessie's heritage, could be applicable beyond the personal
story of Jessie's inability to find "an occasion for loving." It
could be extended to the race problem which forms the major
business of the novel, with its racial hatreds, blood-line terrors
(what in the United States would be called the "tar-brush"
fear), and legal absurdities.

Mrs. Fuecht comes to the Stilwells two days after Bruno's
end becomes known. She "cannot be said to be bereaved" but
Jessie is considerate of her aloneness, at least. The two women
talk practical matters of property and money (the property
had not all been liquidated, after all). Tom sits listening to
them, wondering in pity at the lack of grief in their voices.
Once more, it is the "paid mourner" situation.

One evening he was impelled to ask, "Bruno Fuecht—why did you
never leave him, I often wondered?"

Mrs. Fuecht said without a pause, "I gave him my whole life; I
did not think I could let myself lose his money, as well."

There was a silence; if the jingle of the dinner-bell that Elizabeth
was ringing for Agatha, had not broken it, it might have gone on
forever—there seemed no words that could have ended it. Tom
touched his wife, and she turned, awoke with a strange smile. They
rose like lovers; for lately the sense of strangeness that one being
has for another had come between them.[14]

With these "occasions for loving" in the expertly done book 1
of the novel before us, we are ready for the hedonistic, carefree

love of Ann Davis for her African artist. The occasions so far,
like the loves and marryings in *Pride and Prejudice,* are object
lessons in how not to love, how to manipulate love, how to
misuse love, how to create dry cold where there should be a
warm flowing. The wild, energetic passion of Ann Davis and
a black man, with its vitalism thrust right into the home of Jessie
Stilwell, will gain from its juxtaposition to her coldness.

IV   *Ann Davis*

Ann Davis is an egocentric, careless, opportunistic girl who
confronts life without many long thoughts. She had married
Boaz Davis for adventure, for luck, for the sufficient reason
of escaping the London flat. She was not political, especially,
although she had adopted the currently popular liberal posture
against racial prejudice. She was a help to her husband in
his field work on tribal music; she was responsive and interested in tribal life—but the day's work was sufficient for her;
the next day she could go off with equal aplomb upon another
quite different project.

She was "a nearly beautiful girl" in Jessie's eyes, with eyebrows a bit too thick, and an oddly pointed tooth which one
noticed when she smiled. On her part, she saw in Jessie a
preoccupied, middle-aged woman, "whose face was beginning
to take on the shape of the thoughts and emotions she had
lived through." She saw in Morgan a queer older kid from
an earlier marriage; and in all, a family living in an older
house with not enough money.

She loved being appropriated, rather early on, by a lively
art and drama group. Len Mafolo, an old family friend, was
her liaison to the crowd, but Ann soon abandoned him for
someone more exciting: Gideon Shibolo, a painter and teacher
with "the moody face of a man who pleases everybody but
himself." Gideon takes her to the boxing matches and to other
colorful affairs, and to parties at the homes of his friends, both
white and black. He is a man known and welcomed everywhere.
Ann takes pride in his interest in her, recognizes and welcomes
her sexual power, and likes showing other men that she finds
a black man interesting. When he quite bluntly propositions
her, she says, " 'Why not?' "

Just before this casual, yet urgent response to mutually demanding sexuality, there occurs another of Miss Gordimer's *traits de lumière*, which becomes a conductor of light and validity for the scene following. Ann, racing downstairs to join Gideon, sees Mrs. Fuecht's profile through the open door of the living room. She stops and is drawn to the window where the old woman sits.

"Hullo. All alone?" The girl's face had the blind eagerness of a face in a high wind; nerve endings alive, responses on the surface, like the flash of sun or the shiver of wind on water.

The old woman scarcely existed in the moment. Her carefully powdered face was a mummification of such moments as the girl's; layer on layer, bitumen on bandage, she held the dead shape of passion and vitality in the stretch of thick white flesh, falling from cheekbone to jaw, the straggling but still black eyebrows holding up the lifeless skin round them, and the incision of the mouth. The lips showed only when she spoke, shiny pale under a lash of saliva.

"It seemed I never would be."

The air bridled between them. "Can I get you anything?" said Ann. The old woman smiled. "What?"

"I just wondered—"

"Oh, I know. Now and then one notices other people and is at a loss."

The girl laughed and the old woman took it like a confession. But it was an exchange of confidences: she said, "As time goes by there seems to be more of them—other people. And then, all of a sudden, you're one of them."

Ann sat down on the edge of a small table.

"Weren't you on your way?"

Their eyes met, blank and intimate. She got up. "I'll be going, then." She paused, a bird balancing a moment on a telephone wire. "Good-bye."

The old woman did not change the angle of her head over her book while the front door banged and the clip of heels faded down the path, but when the house was silent again, the alert spread of her nostrils slackened. The silence where the voices of the girl and the unknown man had sounded was the silence within her where many voices were no longer heard.[15]

This event is a vivid irrelevancy, one of the marks of the epiphany, as practiced by Joyce and Flaubert. It resonates with the meaning of events past, and of events to come, in an oblique or metaphorical fashion. It is, in a way, a slice of time (as opposed to a slice of life, which is concerned only with the realistic present). It is vivid in the imagery of vision, in a tableau of youth and old age, passion and death. As it operates here, it is a masterstroke of Miss Gordimer's genius.

Jessie, watching the affair progress, speculates whether Ann is also still sleeping with her husband Boaz and decides that she is, with complete unconcern. Gideon calls at the Stilwell home with "an air of the commonplace, of normality." He has the use of Ann's car; he does some studies of Ann in the nude, sometimes in a black version. Through Gideon's eyes, we get the speculation that, between blacks and whites, "it was easier to have an affair than a friendship." We stay within Gideon's viewpoint, at this stage of the affair, to visit his street, his world:

> The smells of cheap soap, dirty feet, oranges, chips, and the civet smell of perfume on a girl spooky-faced with white women's make-up, soon overcome by the warm, strong sourness of Kaffir beer, given out from the pores of the men and shining on their faces like a libation.[16]

Here he is completely the natural man, no role-playing. With his friend Sol, he goes into the old refrains of politics—the dream of "taking over," of gaining independence from white domination.

The love affair of Ann and Gideon goes into a pleasant routine. They go off for a holiday at Easter while Boaz is on an extended research trip. As it must, it becomes overt. To Jessie, Ann says, " 'You knew, of course?' " Jessie says, " 'Yes,' " and goes on to ask, " 'What's he like?' 'I like him,' " says Ann. There are no dramatic confrontations, of the triangle variety or any other, nor moral issues of any sort.

Ann tells Boaz, finally, that she's been having an affair. The occasion is that Boaz is home, for a change, and Ann feels that she must not stop seeing Gideon just because of that—otherwise it would seem that she was having an affair only because her husband was away—and it has more meaning, she thinks. Boaz takes it calmly. He remarks to Jessie, " 'Ann can't bear threats.

She's always been a pleasure-seeking sort.' " Because he's "not keen on color feeling," Boaz does not make waves of any sort. He'd once slept with a black woman; he can't, even had he been so inclined, bring himself to raise a traditional row, since Gideon is a black man.

Jessie, for her part, does not moralize; she feels sorrow for Boaz, and for Ann, sorrow derived from a sense of the futility in the bondage of sensual compulsion:

How bungling his beauty was, his and Ann's, that had brought them senselessly together and given them the sense of happiness in each other, both to themselves and to onlookers. Take away the running blood, the saliva, the animation of breath, let the beauty harden into its prototypes, and even this would be found something they did not have in common.[17]

This turn-of-the-century Darwinism of the Somerset Maugham stripe is quickly given a counterpoint by another set of human follies. Tom's father comes for a visit. The elder Stilwell had visited once or twice when Len, or other black friends of the Stilwell's, were there. To his cronies later, he had assumed a liberal attitude, preening himself a bit, about the presence of blacks in his son's house. This time he corners Gideon, and gives forth: " 'I've always had a lot of respect for your people. And I've always found them to show respect in return.' " Later, after a couple of gins:

"After all, it's nonsense to talk of marrying and all that—politician's scare talk, I tell people. I'm sure none of us thinks of that. But you can't tell me there's any good reason why you and I shouldn't be having a chat together in a drawing-room, if the mood takes us."[18]

Tom, looking on, is saying under his breath, " 'Oh, Christ.' " Later, Boaz yields to the brandies he's been having all evening, and his liberalism wears thin. He says to Tom:

"If you knew the insane things that've been going on—the whole of tonight—'black bastard'—over and over again to myself, while I was talking—like a maniac—'black bastard.' "[19]

V Gideon's Habitat

Part 2 of the novel closes with Gideon. We follow him to the old part of the city where he grew up. He has a visit with Sandile, his brother-in-law who keeps a shop, and talks of Clara, Gideon's wife whom he had deserted three years ago. Clara wants to come back to him, but that would bring him back to the old township, and he will have none of it. He walks the streets, and we get Miss Gordimer's rich street writing once more, this time applied to thoughts of returning to Clara:

> As he walked out of the shop and along the streets of Alexandra, the naked-bottomed children, the skeletal dogs, the young girls in nylons and the old women who shuffled along under the weight of great buttocks, the decaying rubbish in the streets, the patched and pocked houses, the bicycles shaking as if they would fall apart, the debased attempts at smartening up some hovels that made them look more sordid than those that were left to their rotting-drabness—everything around him spoke of her.[20]

And of course, he rejects it, even though the rich and varied life is more truly himself than the rather shaky white/black role he is presently playing. He goes at last to a political meeting with some of his township friends. Here he has a fixed identity into which he fits comfortably, with the familiar arguments about passive resistance and protest marches, with words that flow easily, like litanies.

VI Jessie at the Beach

Part 3 of the novel opens with Jessie as sojourner, living in a beach cottage with no memories for her—a particular situation which she finds satisfying. She enjoys the genre scene of beach life, the people she sees, all undemanding strangers; the drive to the little store; the Zulus working the sugar-cane alongside the road. She is a woman we have met before in Miss Gordimer's gallery—one who relishes the casual encounter, the quick, perceptive glance, and no consequences.

There had been a discussion about Morgan, before her departure for a holiday at the coast. Tom wanted her to take Morgan along; she had resisted (he's such a bore) and finally she had prevailed. She had left Johannesburg just before Morgan was to arrive from school. Tom, in his letters, mentions him occasionally.

In her constant inventory of self, she notes that she has dropped her habit of composing her face in a mirror, in preparation for encounters, as she had been doing back in Johannesburg. The linear episodes of beach life suit her; she strolls, she observes, she has no involvements. She sun-bathes, she goes for another walk along the beach; she reads Conrad's *Victory*.

Intruding into this cherished oasis come Ann and Gideon. They have been on the road, sleeping in the car, and haven't had a bath in days. They had been to Basutoland, and then to Messina, quickly exhausting the meager hospitality of friends; now they have thought of Jessie and have tracked her down. Jessie gets a *déjà vu* image of the first appearance of Ann and Boaz at her home, an intrusion reluctantly suffered for Tom's sake. " 'How did you find me?' " is her first response. She had "a moment of violent dismay, cringing fiercely from the intrusion."

What did he expect of her, Gideon Shibalo? You always had to do things for them because they were powerless to do anything for you. But did that mean that there was no limit to it, no private demarcation that anyone might be allowed to make before another? Because he has no life here among us, must I give him mine?[21]

Ann and Gideon are to stay only a day or so, but she hasn't the energy for a confrontation, and the few days become a week, then weeks.

The strange slant that Morgan gives to her capacity for love comes in here. Morgan also invades her privacy, and she keeps him on the fringes of her responsiveness, yielding only to a reluctant sense of obligation.

Once, when Gideon is playing with the little girls:

Elizabeth became what was known among them as "cheeky," flinging herself at Gideon, hiding her face so that no one knew whether she was crying or laughing.

"Boy, if my brother was here, he would beat you," Clemence jeered warningly. "Just see if my brother Morgan was here." Jessie

looked at the little girls with a break of curiosity; she had not thought
that Morgan had his place in their scheme of things.[22]

Then again Morgan comes up when she is talking with Tom
on the telephone. They have been talking about the situation
of Ann and Gideon; Tom fears that Ann may be picked up by
the South African police under the immorality laws. He is
dismayed when Jessie tells him that she has finally ordered
them on their way. In the midst of the exchange, Tom says
abruptly:

> "Morgan sends his love." The change in the voice told her that
> the child must have come up and be standing by the phone.
> "Yes, and mine. Don't put him on the phone, I want to talk to you."
> But Morgan's presence with Tom at the other end of the line, and
> the presence of others (she could hear someone moving through the
> living room, on the other side of the door) at her end, made it
> impossible.[23]

Her inability to love Morgan is somehow related to her reaction to the love-making of Ann and Gideon. One time she
blunders into their bedroom and discovers them asleep, naked
under the sheets, all entwined. The informal beach life, the
constant togetherness, forces upon Jessie the very throb of
their sexual play. She resents it, as she resents other intrusions,
but she feels the powerfully inductive warmth, too. Once, she
ruminates, at an earlier time in her life, she might have been
the one sharing the hot, rumpled sheets.

The time on the beach, for all of Jessie's ambivalent response, was a healing time for the fugitive couple. Jessie had
not realized, with their tough coolness, how distressful that
homeless and essentially stateless road life had been. For Ann,
we are soon to discover, it had a delayed effect. Even while
she is making love with Gideon, her self-absorbed decision-
making processes are at work. With the holiday over, in the
car going from the coast up to Johannesburg, the decision is
made, and it is against Gideon.

Back in Johannesburg, life goes on much as before the
holiday. Gideon comes calling, Ann goes out with him; Boaz
is in and out of town. One bleak fall day, Gideon comes calling

and the three: Jessie, Ann, and Gideon, sit before a smoky
fire and talk. They talk about the days at the beach; Jessie has
heard that the neighbors there had complained about "that
black man" on the beach, and making free with the cottage
the Stilwell family occupied; she feels a perverse loyalty to
the lovers. Gideon feels exuberant:

He put his arms around Jessie and held her, and kissing her, said,
"When are you coming up to Tanganyika? Or will it be London? But
Tanganyika's a good place, eh?" But she knew that she would never
see him again.[24]

She knew too that there would never be a Tanganyika, or any
other asylum of freedom for Gideon and Ann; and it is because of Ann.

The Davises have already decided that they must return to
Europe. Boaz has "hardened in the only way possible to
someone of his still inert nature," by holding himself off from
events a little more. Ann had put the whole affair behind her
with no dramatics. " 'She says everyone has had enough,' "
Boaz reports of her. She has not told Gideon.

With Ann gone, Gideon begins drinking, and is seen about
town, always drunk. Jessie is distressed; but Tom maintains
sardonically that he would have started drinking if they *had*
stayed together. He says, pragmatically:

"What could the bloody woman do, if she didn't want him, or
couldn't face wanting him?"
"Nothing," said Jessie. "Nothing. She's white, she could go, and
of course she went."

They came again and again to the stony silence of facts they had
set their lives against. They believed in the integrity of personal re-
lations against the distortions of laws and society. What stronger
and more proudly personal bond was there than love? Yet even
between lovers they had seen blackness count, the personal return
inevitably to the social, the private to the political.

So long as the law remained unchanged, nothing could bring integrity to personal relationships.

The Stilwells' code of behavior, like their marriage, was definitive,
like their marriage; they could not change it. But they saw that it was
a failure, in danger of humbug. Tom began to think there would be

more sense in blowing up a power station; but it would be Jessie who would help someone to do it, perhaps in time.[25]

Jessie sees Gideon again, at a party; he has been drinking heavily, before and during the party. He is in the company, or perhaps custody, of a large black girl. Jessie approaches him, putting aside the apprehension that he may not care to see one of the Stilwells. He is too drunk to recognize her. He mumbles, " 'Get away, white bitch.' "

Jessie tells Tom of the incident, and asks, " 'What's going to happen to him?' " Tom says, " 'He'll go back and fight; there's nothing else.' " And with this old proletarian slogan, the novel closes.

I once heard Miss Gordimer, in a lecture, discussing Sarah Gertrude Millin's *God's Stepchildren*, in which an interracial marriage and the production of children of mixed blood is a major issue, the Dostoevskian sense of sin. Near the end of the book, a young English wife, upon hearing the confession of mixed blood, says, " 'Is that all?' " Miss Gordimer, commenting upon that three word put-down, goes on to say:

> The cat is out of the bag, for the nation and the novel. Is that all? Is that the stuff of sin? Is that the stuff of tragedy? And if it is, at what a curious disadvantage must it put us with the peoples of other nations, whose writers are concerned with man's survival and the meaning of his life on earth.[26]

I wish that Miss Gordimer had kept her critical precepts in mind before giving us such pompous nonsense as "So long as the law remained unchanged, nothing could bring integrity to personal relationships," and the further line, equally nonsensical: "Tom began to think there would be more sense in blowing up a power station; but it would be Jessie who would help someone do it, perhaps in time." Most readers, I am sure, would have difficulty visualizing Jessie doing any such thing. Her cold dryness toward Morgan, her low-profile love for Tom, her apparent forgetfulness for pages on end that she has three little girls do not indicate any such passion for justice or for the wronged lovers.

Before getting deeper into nit-picking, understandable though

such an impulse may be as a symptom of deep reader dis-
satisfaction with the resolution of the novel, let us look for
trouble earlier on.

The novel is a fascinating failure—fascinating because of
the superb writing in book 1. Miss Gordimer's creation of the
relationship of Morgan and his mother is beautiful; it has a
bitter acridity about it, a puzzlingly motivated but very believable situation about which Jessie feels contrite but also self-
justifying. She must first be true to herself, to Tom, to her
new family, or so she tells herself. Yet that is not all of it;
she is helplessly distant and cold to the very appealing boy.
He is a masterpiece of mid-teen ineptness, of the terrible
need for recognition and approval—and he gets none. This is
a beautiful, energetic, fruitful idea for the novel; yet little or
no use is made of it. One almost feels that it belongs in a
different novel—perhaps one written by Henry James or Peter
Taylor (neither of whom, by the way, would be sucked into
the racial and social statements that resolve this novel).

Because of the *données* of the author about Jessie, and the
character qualities given to Ann, one never accepts the love-
making as any more than a holiday game, on both sides, although
we are required to accept the idea that Gideon was more
serious than Ann. I believe in neither; hence the weighty value
given it by Jessie (tragic lovers separated by the unjust policies
of society) is nowhere supported.

The difficulties in the last part of the novel arise from several
sources. One is that the major plot element—the lovers separated—is an essentially romantic one. Whether the separation
is to come about because of feuding families, social status,
race, or great peoples in the chaos of war, we first have to
believe in the lovers *as* lovers. Their love must approach the
fervor of a secular religion. To mix in sociological or psychological realism—the realism of the social studies—is to turn
Romeo and Juliet over to a board of marriage counselors and
send Dr. Zhivago to the couch.

Another source of difficulty arises, paradoxically, out of the
fine writing of book 1. The novel, which moves into the category
of Problem Novel, particularly in the last book, is similar in
its social posturings to the proletarian novels of the thirties

and forties. To point the finger of social blame most tellingly, with the implied solution of some sort of social engineering for the dilemmas presented, the authors of the social problem novels created the simplest of characters: no traits of envy or pride, no divided man at war with himself, no irony. Thus, when disaster struck, the cause was clearly visible—as was the solution ("blow up the power station"). The trouble here is that the writing is too good; the characters are too complex. We want Jessie to be "true" to the character created for her; that is, to make functional use, in the novel, of those fascinating qualities we become involved in early on.

It may be that "race" is the dominating subject for any South African novelist writing of that society today, as Miss Gordimer said in the same lecture I referred to earlier. I disagree, but suppose for the moment that it be true. Then Miss Gordimer must do in her novel what she has done so masterfully in her best short stories concerning race—let it strike tangentially upon interesting and complex situations already holding our absorbed attention. Specifically, this means that the Jessie we come to know early in the novel, and her relationship to Morgan, must continue to function and grow, as touched by race energies that modify and reveal latent thrusts. Instead, Jessie becomes an under-used instrument for viewing Ann and Gideon who aren't really worth it and Morgan is very nearly discarded after his touching, appealing, provocative appearances in book 1.

CHAPTER 8

The Late Bourgeois World

*T*HE *Late Bourgeois World*[1] is a short *tour de force*, a
    novella rather than a novel. It gives us one day in the
life of Elizabeth Van Den Sandt, during which she receives
word of the death by suicide of her traitorous ex-husband, Max;
visits a boys school to tell her son of the death of his father;
goes to see her senile grandmother, now in a nursing home; has
a short visit from her current lover; and at the last has an
evening with a black activist who wishes to get her assistance
in the movement. The story is told with many time-shifts, during
which we get episodes in her life with Max, early in-law problems, and glimpses of the South African resistance movement of
the 1950's and 1960's.

If one were to conjure up the image of the author, near the end
of a career, looking once more at the collected works, he could
imagine Miss Gordimer smiling nostalgically and fondly at the
tender innocence of *The Lying Days*; ruefully leafing through
the first real try at the novel, *A World of Strangers*, with its
unsteady male viewpoint and bald political rhetoric; look with
some pride at *Occasion for Loving* and its "chance missed"
but considerable success for all that; and then come to *The Late
Bourgeois World*. This one would be put aside with an embarrassed wince for exclusion, perhaps, from the collected works,
and the reasons are many.

Some of these reasons have to do with warmed-over materials:
once more we have the woman in an odd, cold relationship with
a teenage son from a past marriage, once more disposed of in
a boys school; once more we have the establishment figures
drawn with such angry disdain that they become cartoons; once
more, after the cold dryness of relationships with whites—
lovers, friends, husbands, sons—we have the warm vitalism of

135

the black man, with laughter, wine, delicious food, and exciting talk.

But, beyond these familiar encounters, we have in this novel a particularly embarrassing failure—again a point-of-view problem—in the woman protagonist. Elizabeth, the woman in her thirties telling the story, has the swaggering bravado of a teenage rebel. How she could have supposedly lived through the events of her life and remained the tiresome adolescent she is, boggles the mind. Witness a few moments: here she is, explaining the careers of her current lover, a liberal lawyer named Graham, and herself:

Graham defends many people on political charges and is one of a handful of advocates who ignore the possible consequences of getting a reputation for being willing to take such cases. I've got my job analysing stools for tapeworm and urine for bilharzia and blood for cholesterol (at the Institute for Medical Research). And so we keep our hands clean. So far as work is concerned, at least. Neither of us makes money out of cheap labour or performs a service confined to people of a particular colour. For myself, thank God, shit and blood are all the same, no matter whom they come from.[2]

(Lighting a cigarette, to hide the quick look at the listener's hoped-for shock reaction to that last—my parenthesis.) And, the listener, still looking for the kind of intelligence displayed in "A Bit of Young Life" might, with the teasing wickedness of Lear's fool, say, "That last batch of feces, I happen to know, came from a rich merchant of Johannesburg—what then?"

Another bit of swagger, to give further samples of this impossible smart-mouth, occurs when she is describing her relationship with Graham, her lover: "Graham and I have no private names, references, or love-words. We use the standard vocabulary, when necessary."[3] "Standard vocabulary when necessary" must mean unisex candor in sexual exchanges, with the bold use of four-letter words, of course.

Role-playing "candor" again comes into Elizabeth's description of a bedroom scene with Graham, done with all the "candor" of an adolescent posing for pornographic pictures while parents are away for the weekend:

He's much better than someone my own age, he comes to me with a solid and majestic erection that will last as long as we choose. Sometimes he will be in me for an hour and I can put my hand on my belly and feel the blunt head, through my flesh.[4]

Good God, says the reader, cringing at the adolescent bravado masquerading as "candor." How can I believe this narrator upon any of the subjects in the novel: racial justice, white liberalism, revolutionary resistance, or any other endeavor, be it personal, social, or political?

The difficulties put in the way of the reader by this sort of narrator obscure the meaning of events, and interfere with the very necessary empathy of the reader. However, a narrator who sees events through a properly obscured viewpiece, as do the narrators in Ford Madox Ford's *The Good Soldier*, or the various narrators in Henry James's *The Golden Bowl*, to cite only two among many, may enhance the reader's experience. The short-story genre is replete with such treatments, often stunningly successful. Miss Gordimer, as we have noted, has had such successes in the short story, upon occasion.

Viewpoint manipulation must be done in such a way as to intrigue the reader, not repel him. If properly done, he will be pulled into the story, with the illusion of living the story himself, so diligently has his imagination worked to see through this "wrong" telling. That effect occurs when the narrative viewpoint is "wrong," not *wrong*. A beautiful instance of the way it should work is the viewpoint of Humbert Humbert in *Lolita*. Humbert is stubbornly romantic, completely self-delusive about the truth, and the reader takes delight in seeing through Humbert's telling.

When Conrad, or James, or Huxley is creating his viewpoint character, he does so with careful consideration of the subject-matter to be so viewed. Maggie's viewpoint in *The Golden Bowl* comes late in the book, not early, because the fall from innocence in the major alliances must be established first before we get events from her particular kind of innocence in a state of change to a tougher maturity. Her qualities illuminate, create shadows in one place and bold relief in another—all under the careful control of the master artist. Lolita's earthy acceptance of the events of her young life and her relationship with the romantic Humbert help to dictate the quality of Humbert's mistaken viewing.

When we peer more closely at Max Van Den Sandt, whose suicide we discover early in the first chapter, we find a potentially fascinating character whose qualities are not illuminated by the manner of viewing; they are in fact hidden from us by the disdain and vindictiveness of the viewing character. He is the son of a South African M.P., well-to-do, well-educated, engaging, nurtured in a *haute bourgeoisie* life. Young Elizabeth discovers that she is pregnant, so she and Max must marry rather in haste. Elizabeth discovers that she has married the Van Den Sandt family, made even more distasteful because of early economic dependence. Max's mother, who affects a rather rich "English country" life style, is fond of saying, " 'I'm just a Boer girl, you know. I must go out and get my feet dirty among the mealies now and then.' " She speaks Xhosa to the household menservants, whom she attires in starched white uniforms with red sashes. She has a Cape colored cook, with whom she talks Afrikaans in amiable conversation. Somehow these are marks against her.

Mr. Van Den Sandt, a small man with a red face and stiff hair, came from an English emigrant family. Gold mining and politics had put him where he was, and we cannot forgive his self-made affluence, nor his friends:

lobbying for support of Bills that would have the effect of lowering or raising the bank rate, on which they depended for their investments, industrial Bills on which they depended for their cheap labour, or land apportionment on which they depended to keep the best for themselves.[5]

The Van Den Sandts, despite their Philistinism, take the prenuptial pregnancy in stride, for which they get little thanks from Elizabeth. Mrs. Van Den Sandt says:

"It's just a *mistake*, that's all," in a sort of soothing baby-talk, as if a puppy had wet the carpet. And after Max and I were married, she looked at me with mock censure, raising her eyebrows and smiling when we came to lunch one day: "Oh, *look* at its little belly, if you please. My dear, all the old cats are going to start counting soon—but we don't care a fig for them, do we!"[6]

Not bad for a rather conventionally reared older generation, would be my assessment. Not Elizabeth. She despises them; and her venom is of course based upon their being on the wrong side of the ideological fence.

The parents do not know that the young couple is being titillated by the resistance movement; that Max is spending his time in ghettos with African and Indian activists. The Van Den Sandts "must have relied on me to lead Max by the penis, as it were, into the life he was born for"; and of course it was a foolish trust. The crisis comes when Max joins a Communist cell, takes part in a Defiance Campaign march, and is put in jail. The charges against him are later dropped, probably through his father's influence as an M.P. Then Max makes a bomb, not a successful one, but enough to get him tried on a charge of sabotage.

For the Van Den Sandts, their son was dead to them from that moment, says the narrator. But we find that the father made money available for his defense, and his mother attended the trial. His father resigned his seat in Parliament, and refused to be present at the trial. Elizabeth has an obnoxious encounter with Mrs. Van Den Sandt in a corridor outside the courtroom:

At the recess, as we all clattered into the echoing corridors of the courts, I smelt her perfume. People talking as they went, forming groups that obstructed each other, had squeezed us together. The jar of coming face to face opened her mouth after years of silence between us. She spoke, "What have we done to deserve this!" Under each eye and from lips to chin were deep scores, like lashes of a beauty's battle with age. I came back at her—I don't know where it came from—"You remember when he burned his father's clothes."

Footsteps rang all about us, we were being jostled.

"What? All children get up to things. That was nothing."

"He did it because he was in trouble in school, and he'd tried to talk to his father for days, but his father was too busy. Every time he tried to lead round to what he wanted to say he was told, run away now, your father's busy."

Her painted mouth shaped an incredulous laugh. "What are you talking about?"

"Yes, you don't remember. But you'll remember it was the time when your husband was angling to get into the cabinet. The time when he wanted to be Chief Whip, and was so busy."

I was excited with hatred of her self-pity, the very smell of her stank in my nostrils.[7]

The incredulity might very well be the reader's: at the "painted lips shaped an incredulous laugh" gaucherie, at the cut-rate psychological motivation, which the reader knows to be a cheap shot, since he has had insights into the real nature of the narrator's hatred. Motivation, it might be said in an aside, is much overrated for creating validity in scene or character. A quick glance at Iago will prove the point; he is one of the most valid, complete, fascinating characters in all of literature, and his scenes are utterly compelling. What was his motivation? Echo answers. To get back to the "painted lips" for a moment; we get them again when we visit an aged grandmother in the nursing home.

After the trial, and for some months in prison, Max has the uneasy status of hero to the mercurial group of radicals. His dilemma approximates that of Razumov in Conrad's *Under Western Eyes*, apparently—that torment is untold—for after some months he turns state's evidence and is released. Then he has nobody: no parents, no activist friends, and soon, no wife.

The story of Max, the very model of the political activist, is the South African version—well-educated, from middle, or upper-middle class, devoted—of the same mold that produced John Reed, young John Dos Passos, Frederich Engels, and many another, that story is lost here because of viewpoint management. It is a story that needs telling, one that would bring sympathy and understanding to a well-deserved cause; instead we get the objective gamine wife, and her dry, cool life.

Max was fifteen months in prison after his trial for sabotage, before he decided to turn state's evidence. During that time he had his "Darkness at Noon" in which he came to some truths—for him—about his activities and his friends. To call him coward or unequal to stern demands is an easy way out.

His change of heart, properly perceived, is the heart of a novel, here another "chance missed."

It was for radical dilettantism, and for his defection, that Elizabeth abandoned him, although she doesn't specify. It was not the various women in his life—poor Felicity of the big, quaking breasts, or beautiful Roberta. Her venom is reserved, not for sexual adventures, for she has her own, but for political adventurism. After his trial, and for the fifteen months of his imprisonment before he became a turncoat, we may presume that he had Elizabeth's approval, although that period is not detailed. Max was a dillettante; he entered in the movement to *be* somebody, not for the cause of the people—or so Elizabeth saw him, as her disenchantment grew. She became sure that the people (meaning blacks) meant as little to him as to his parents. He associated with them, of course, but he was using them, and they felt it.

Before the book closes with a visit from the vital, healthy Luke Fogase, a black activist very much in the front lines of the battle, we make a visit to a nursing home to see Elizabeth's grandmother. It serves as another counterpoint event, to bring back the meaningless days as a girl in her parents' shop, her early marriage to Max, the growing hatred of the bourgeoisie, and finally the escape.

In the course of reminiscing while visiting grandmother, we discover that Elizabeth had hated working in her father's shop, hated the shoddy goods palmed off on the innocents and her part in the shameful business; then the "sickening secret" of Max's family life:

that this quality of life was apparently what our fathers and grandfathers had fought two wars abroad and killed black men in "native wars" of conquest here at home, to secure for us. Truth and beauty—good God, that's what I thought he would find, that's what I expected of Max.[8]

What kept the two together, so far as we may surmise, was political affinity, which meant mostly having disdain for the same things. When the scales fell from Elizabeth's eyes about Max's devotion to the cause of the blacks, she had nothing but hatred for him, plus a feeling of contempt. At news of his death,

beyond vivid images of what it would be like to die by drown-
ing in a car driven into the harbour, she gives no thought to his
death—no sorrow, no pity, no grief.

At the end of her day, her lover Graham comes calling while
she is preparing dinner for a visitor. She had lied to him about
her evening plans. They talk about the American space-walk,
also taking place on this day of death-for-Max; and about the
spectacular sunset "possibly from fallout." They begin having
what Graham calls an "undergraduate talk," and the phrase
brings a defensiveness to Elizabeth's thoughts:

Even though I know I'm a damned intelligent woman—by far the
most intelligent female he's ever had any sort of dealings with—and
that a relationship with a woman of my kind implies the acceptance
not only of intellectual equality but also coeval commonsense (none
of the patronizing affection towards precocious feminine cleverness)—
in spite of this, now when I'm holding up my end in discussion a
shade better than he is, there's a sort of backwards glance in me, at
my performance before him.[9]

In the interchange of ideas, Graham says abruptly, "What about
us?" And the probability develops that this cool and rather
clinical sexual accommodation will terminate.

With Graham gone, Elizabeth hastens preparations for her
African visitor, Luke Fokase. He was not one of the "old crowd"
when Max was still active, but he'd been to the house a time
or two. She found him interesting; in truth, the phrase, "immensely charming" applies more aptly. The vitality of events
quickens upon the appearance of Luke, a "large, grinning young
man" with "enormous almond eyes that were set in their wide-
spaced openings in the black skin like the painted eyes of smiling Etruscan figures." Luke embraces her familiarly, with "a
little appraising lift, with the heel of the hand, on the outer
sides of my breasts, as one says, 'There' " and the two drift into
the living room. They talk of politics, of the past; they have
brandy; delicious odors come from the kitchen. "Our voices
rose and we were laughing," the only joyous laughter in the
book. They sit down to dinner and eat their food with gusto—
the only gusto in the book.

She announces, off-hand, that her ex-husband is dead; and she won't be going to the funeral. She says, casually:

"If he'd been one of your chaps he wouldn't have needed to do it, ay? Someone else would have stuck a knife in him and thrown him in the harbour."[10]

The talk of Max is soon dropped, and we get back to the main business of the evening, which, besides teasing love-making, is to get Elizabeth to find some money to support the movement. Just that week, twenty-one more have been charged with sabotage, and money is needed for their defense.

As they talk, she thinks of her grandmother's account, for which she has power of attorney to make payments to the nursing home and meet other expenses—and it's all just being wasted on the futile costs of senility:

And while we talked, the thought was growing inside me, almost like sexual tumescence, and like it—I was nervous—perhaps communicating its tension.[11]

She promises to see what she can do, and after Luke has gone and she is in bed, she lies awake. She thinks about the Americans, alive in space above her; about Max, floating in his watery grave; about Luke and how he'll probably come back, when his excellent sense of timing tells him to come. How he'll probably make love to her; and about the checkbook on grandmother's account, within easy reach of her hand.

The difficulty in this short, hastily written and journalistic novel is the author's failure to hold the camera steady. Her viewing character comes through as a particularly disagreeable sexual and political adolescent. Was that the author's intention? After all, viewing events through a biased, bigoted, sentimental —or what have you—character is a valid, and often stunning, fictional method.

I can't believe that it *was* the author's intention; the finished product has too much aborted, too much awry. In the political controversy implicit in the novel, the establishment figures appear as caricatures, stupid cartoons who are an offense to the reader's intelligence—particularly to the reader who has read some of Miss Gordimer's other work with helpless admiration. The use of such a viewing character likewise makes sentimentalized caricatures of the "good guys" of her story—no benefit either to their credibility or to the political cause they espouse. In her latest novel, *A Guest of Honour*, Miss Gordimer manages her adversaries much more adroitly and convincingly.

But in this one, most unfortunately of all, Max is lost to the reader. His story could give profundity, even tragedy to the South African scene—and writing capable of rising above melodama to tragedy is badly needed there. Max is not merely a victim; he is "author of his woe"; he becomes universally despised, and self-despising. His story deserves more than a cartoon strip, however beautifully styled.

So the novel, in a final word, is another "chance missed." Why should it come out that way: political stridency? Settling some personal scores? For whatever reasons, Miss Gordimer has done what she so adroitly avoids in her most beautiful short stories: namely, let her political views cloud her vision, with this unfortunate result.

CHAPTER 9

A Guest of Honour

M ISS Gordimer's most recent novel, her fifth, A *Guest of Honour*,[1] is notable on several counts. It is her first novel about an African country other than South Africa. It is the first novel examining the political life in a new African nation following independence. It is the first time we have blacks against blacks in the conflict arena, a most significant difference. Finally, and related, it is the first truly mature, substantial, well-made novel of the five. Although Miss Gordimer's political alliances are visible here as well, the alignment of "good guys" versus "bad guys" has disappeared. Blacks are also, we discover, capable of dirty politics—even murderous politics—and they are also greedy for power and are ruthless and deceitful in its pursuit; they also violate civil liberties and rig the police and the courts; they also betray former comrades in obedience to a "new reality." The novel tells us these things—certainly not new to any follower of the news from Africa in the last ten years—with a sadness, a weariness almost, of truths reluctantly acknowledged.

Miss Gordimer tries a male protagonist once more, this time with far greater success than before. Colonel James Evelyn Bray is the "guest of honour," invited back to the African country from which he had been officially ejected ten years before. He had been District Commissioner, a position which embraces the duties of policeman, judge, agricultural agent, local representative of His Majesty's government—in short, for his district he is God. Because he had been thought too sympathetic to the PIP (People's Independent Party), he had been removed under pressure from the white establishment. Now the independence movement has succeeded; the former rebels have become the political masters of the new state; and Bray

145

has been invited back as an "honoured guest" of Independence Day celebrations.

From the outset, Bray gives the impression of being a responder, a receptor rather than an energizer. If this were a Graham Greene novel, we would call him a "burned-out case." He is a man who "finds himself" in this or that situation, rather than one who creates and causes situations.

His wife Olivia, who will not accompany him, has a premonition on the eve of Bray's departure:

> In the scented, mothy evening, she felt the presence of the house like someone standing behind her. She did not know whether he felt it too; and she could not try to find out because if it turned out that he didn't—she had a premonition, sometimes, that in middle age you could find that you had lost everything in a moment: husband-lover, friend, children, it was as if they had never happened, or you had wandered off from them without knowing, and now stood stock-still with the discovery.[2]

Bray does take up a new life in Africa, as if this place were the only one where life could exist for him; and thoughts of Olivia and the children become very intermittent and dim.

Upon his arrival, Colonel Bray is taken in charge by a young black man in sunglasses, guided efficiently through customs, and taken to a car. Pictures of President Mweta, his old friend in the Independence struggle, are on every wall; he hears rapid-fire accounts of new factories and of better roads. But he takes greater pleasure in the old scenes they pass, as they go into town from the airport:

> Near the bridge the women were going for water with paraffin tins on their heads. Advertising hoardings had gone up; there was a cement works, smart factories put together out of jutting glassy sections, and in between the patches scratched in the bush where women and children were hoeing crooked rows of beans and maize. The children (an excuse to dawdle, of course) stopped and waved. He found himself waving back urgently, bending his head under the low roof of the car, smiling and craning to hold their faces when they were already out of sight.[3]

He yearns, in the days of ceremony in the capital, for his old district up-country where he can talk to the ancients in their own dialect, and feel the slow pulse of the country he had known. For now, he is committed to a tiresome round of banquets, speeches, and ceremonial events.

For "the man who comes back," he is staying temporarily with a very useful friend. Roland Dando, Attorney General of the new state, and an old friend, is not only bubbling recklessly with gossip, but unlike the new, self-conscious official he uses the old vocabulary, that of colonial days, with which Bray is familiar. Dando "could say what he liked." He hadn't "discovered the blacks only yesterday." He is full of disdain for the black bureaucracy, the "heroes of the struggle" rewarded. Of the lot, Edward Shinza is the only genuine hero, who got his head bashed by His Majesty's troops, and who did his stretch in prison—and where is he? Back in the bush, and no one even mentions his name. Bray is troubled by that news. Shinza has been one of the stalwarts; in fact, Shinza, Bray, and Mweta had formed a zealous, and ultimately successful triumvirate in the fight for independence.

As the action of the novel moves on and Bray finds himself, whether he likes it or not, aligned with the new "black masters" who have replaced the old colonial "white masters," he begins to see in the still idealistic, still rebellious Shinza, a facet of his better self—his lost self whose rebirth costs him his life, as it turns out. For now, he picks up gossip about old friends. A few have stayed on, managing to adapt to the new regime; some had left, but have now returned; some have gone south to Rhodesia or South Africa. And, the gossip has it, Bray has been brought back for more than ceremonial honors; he is to be offered a post, perhaps in the ministry of Education. He is intrigued and flattered.

Ceremonies occupy us for the moment: a State Ball, dinners, receptions, cocktail parties, luncheons. We get a kaleidoscope of quick shots, Nadine Gordimer at the sort of thing she does brilliantly:

A slim white girl slipped between them and took up Ras Asahe's hand with the gold-metal watch bracelet as if it were some possession she had put down. . . . the girl was there in the conversation like a photograph come upon lying between the pages of a book. . . . the girl sat and saw nothing, like an animal out of breath, holed up against danger.[4]

A bit later, Bray finds himself with a big West African woman:

—in her flamboyant national dress, dragged round her as if snatched straight from the brilliant bolt on a shop counter, she seemed in every way twice the size of the local African women, who were usually kept at home, and showed it. . . . She had the self-confidence of a woman of dynamic ugliness.[5]

But nowhere, in this stream of random reality, is there any sign of Shinza. No one seemed to have seen him, and a reluctance to talk about him was noticeable.

Bray does meet, in these first days, a young woman out of Dos Passos's *USA*—a useful, unassuming, errand-runner, girl-of-all-trades "like a big, untidy schoolgirl in her cotton shirt and sandals." A little later, she is to turn up in Gala, Bray's old district, and is to become, with no preliminaries and no complications, his mistress.

At a luncheon with his old friend, President Mweta, the rumors of an appointment are confirmed, as are Bray's growing suspicions. Before Mweta appears, Bray is met by a bright young white man who had been a PRO for one of the mining corporations. His job, it seems, is to protect Mweta from former comrades who think they can just walk in, sit down, and chat, as in the old days. Mweta appears, in a Party tunic ("somewhere between a Mao blouse and a bush jacket"). They reminisce about the old days—ominously with no mention of Edward Shinza.

As they talk, Joy Mweta and the children come in, and for awhile all is laughter, children romping, a heart-warming family gathering. Then an Englishwoman's imperious voice establishes order, to Bray's displeasure. The author's tiny fangs appear at this remnant of the British raj: "Like many women, she bore the date of her vintage year in the manner of her make-up: the pencil-line of the Dietrich eyebrows on the bald fine English skin above each blue eye, the well-powdered nose and fuchsia pink mouth."[6] Her high, clear, "Englishwoman's voice" quickly cuts down the children's boisterous behavior, and the party goes in to lunch. " 'You're not letting that Mrs. Whatnot run the place?' " Bray asks Joy accusingly. It is a trivial incident, but it nags at Bray's sensitive receptors, coming as it does, jarring the naturalness of family life which he had enjoyed. Added to the protocol, the exclusion of old comrades, and the unwillingness to discuss Edward Shinza, it creates discomfort.

Finally, after luncheon, he brings Shinza's name out into the open. Mweta dissimulates. He can't offer Shinza a position in the government—an under-secretaryship would be below him, and he wouldn't accept it. How about something more important, Bray presses. It comes reluctantly out: Shinza wants the revolution to go on; he wants, says Mweta, to change the world, and use their country as the tinder. Bray discounts some of this as rhetoric, and in a reasonable tone says, " 'You talk as if he'd started a rival party.' " Mweta concedes, yes, that was his concern. Shinza has a powerful following, particularly among the unions. More rhetoric, the gist of which is that an opposition party is not to be tolerated, at least not at this time of transition.

II *To Gala, the Old District*

Part 2 of the novel takes us to Gala, Bray's old district on the northern boundary of the country. The tone of the novel changes immediately. Instead of waspish commentary upon the vanity fair of the capital—the readiness of the blacks to reinstall the worst practices of their white predecessors, the court intrigues—we have the serenity of pastoral countryside and the innocence of rural people.

Bray's true homecoming is keyed by the meeting with a country schoolmaster, shyly delighted to be addressed in Gala and in the form of respectful address a pupil might use to a teacher. The schoolmaster introduces a smiling young woman, his wife, who teaches first and second grade and is the choir director. Bray must hear the children sing, and he listens courteously, thinking of the many times he has listened to the children of Gala sing. The schoolmaster speaks of his problems— getting the parents interested, so the children will come with regularity; the need for training in crafts. It is a warming and nourishing encounter for Bray. Now he is glad that he agreed to stay.

We are then treated to some vivid casual encounters, in the brilliant Nadine Gordimer manner. Here, characteristically, is the hotelkeeper:

> Her big head of thick, reddish-blond hair had been allowed to fade to the yellow-stained white of an old man's mustache. She looked up over her glasses and then took them off and got to her feet with the pigeon-toed gait of heavy, ageing women. "I thought it sounded like you, when the boy told me." Sex had died out of the challenging way she had had with men; it was bluff and grudging. They had never liked each other much, in the little they had known of each other, and extraordinarily, the old attitude fell into place between them as if ten years didn't exist. There was laughter and handshaking. "A big *bwana* with grey hair at the sides, and he can talk Gala. . . ."[7]

The vitality of old distaste enlivens their talk. The beautiful lines, "They had never liked each other much, in the little they had known of each other, and extraordinarily the old attitude fell into place between them as if ten years didn't exist" are as splendidly conceived as any Miss Gordimer ever produced. The trouble is, the beauty of such moments creates obligations not met in the major characters or in the larger structures. However, let us enjoy gems where we find them. The conversation with the hotelkeeper goes on; she berates the new regime for its many inane regulations, the forms she must fill out, the permissions she must obtain.

> He said, "I can sympathize. It must be difficult for you."
> She didn't believe him; it was all very well for people like him who hadn't had to make a living, who were sent out by the British government for a few years and took sides with the blacks because they didn't have to stay and live with them if they didn't want to.[8]

Isn't she beautiful? This totally real scene goes on in much more detail, to the delight of the reader, with its acrid edge of disagreement and its bluff humor. An "enticement of insult," as Miss Gordimer puts it. The hotelkeeper tells much news of the district: who has sold up and who plans to; who sold up several years ago and now plans to come back, and the sort of surprise he's in for.

The shy schoolmaster comes to call after dinner, and Bray outlines one of his programs: to get the missionary schools to give over control to the government, but to persuade the teachers to stay on. Even if that succeeds, more teachers will have to be recruited, particularly for crafts, and more schools will have to be built. Bray enjoys the talk and the feeling that he is beginning to function usefully for the country.

He settles into the house provided for him, and his old Africa comes back: "All, immediate, as with the scent of a woman with whom one has made love."[9] A clue to Bray's temperamental commitments comes when he takes a tour of the town; not the new developments, but the old town which he remembered from his years as District Commissioner:

> The old town was filthy and beautiful; in this low-lying ground palms grew, giving their soaring proportions to the huddle, and lifting the skyline to their pure and lazy silhouette. The place stank of beer, ordure, and smoke. The most wretched huddle had its setting of sheeny banana leaves, with a show of plenty in the green candelabra of pendant fruit, and its paw-paw trees as full of ripening dugs as some Indian goddess. Green grew and tangled everywhere out of the muck, rippled and draped over rotting wood and rusting iron. Romantic poverty; he would rather live here, with the rats under the palm trees, than up on the rise in those mean, decent cubes already stained with bare earth; that was because he would never have to live with either. A little naked boy waved with one hand, clutching his genitals with the other. An old man took off his hat in greeting. Bray knew no one and knew them all. There was an anonymity of mutual acceptance that came to him not at all in England, and hardly ever in Europe—in Spain perhaps on market mornings among the butting bodies and smiles of busy people whose language he didn't speak. It wasn't losing oneself, it was finding one's presence so simply that one forgot that outwardly one moved as a large, pink-faced Englishman, light-eyed and thick eyebrowed behind the magnification of glasses.[10]

Unwittingly, Bray has endorsed the hotelkeeper's assessment that "he wouldn't have to live here" so he can pursue his romantic idealism; this is to lead him toward the rebel Shinza and the unrealized dream of the old revolutionary days. But, of course, he doesn't understand the realities of Shinza's program either.

III *A Proletarian Love*

Before long, to reinforce this feeling of innocence, naturalness and goodness in the people, rejoicing in the sense of function and purpose among them, he is to enter into an undemanding and uncomplicated sleeping arrangement with Rebecca. Rebecca has been assigned as secretary to Aleke, the black man who has Bray's old job, now titled Provincial Officer instead of District Commissioner.

To add to Bray's heartwarming sequences of coming home, his old servant, Kalimo, walks a thousand miles to be with him again. Somehow, in African fashion, news reached him, and he has come to look after his Colonel.

Another old friend comes into the story: George Boxer, a white settler who, unlike most of the others, was nonpolitical. He had not taken part in Bray's ouster ten years before. He is a dedicated agronomist; he studies native grasses, tries to find a way to control cattle ticks, and steers clear of district politics. Bray thinks he may be able to draft Boxer to help set up extension courses in agriculture for the black farmers.

The tenor of idyllic return changes soon, however. On his way up-country to try to find Edward Shinza, Bray picks up a taciturn black, a young man with a shaved head—just out of prison, it later emerges, bearing scars of brutal beatings. Bray discovers that the beatings were politically motivated: he is one of "Shinza's boys" and his jailers were seeking information on Shinza's operations.

IV *Shinza, At Last*

He does meet Shinza, after much difficulty. The reunion is a puzzling one. Shinza is edgy, occasionally taunting. Word has preceded Bray, of course, that he is one of Mweta's men. Shinza —American-educated, world-traveled, still young—had been the intellectual of the Independence Party. He looks at Bray in bitter amusement: " 'So you're helping to build a nation, ay?' "

Shinza knows all about Bray's young hitchhiker; it is he who tells the history of the incident and has the young man brought in to show his scars. The overt incident had been the arrangement of a meeting with workers at the fish-meal factory; an informer had relayed the information to the capital. Bray is outraged and intends to take some action. " 'It's possible Mweta doesn't know about it,' " he offers. Shinza smiled in disgusted amusement.

Back in Gala, Bray raises the issue with Aleke, who already knows all about it. It seems the police had orders to make him talk—orders direct from the capital. Even more ominous for Bray's idealistic dreams, a detention act, in the South African mode, has been put into effect while he was up-country. He hastens to see Mweta, is met with a warm handshake and a soporific smile; but the firm statement, " 'I'm not going to stand by and let this country be ruined by troublemakers.' "

Bray's rebuttal is, " 'If you'd given him a ministry, there'd have been no trouble.' " He gets the other side. If Shinza believes that Mweta is perpetuating white man's rule, with a mere change of color in the *bwana*, Mweta believes that Shinza cannot realize that the rebellion is over. " 'He made up his mind he had to watch the rest of us the way he watched *them*.' "

Bray leaves with the impasse unresolved. Later he discovers that the Gala chief of police had been transferred because of Bray's report on the beating. Ironically, this does Bray no good— it merely proves to Shinza and others that he really is Mweta's man, with a powerful pipeline to the throne.

These political plots, with the web tightening around Bray, are Nadine Gordimer the essayist. For long pages, polemics are the concern, with characterization and imagery forgotten. Only the reader interested in political pragmatism could stay interested; for him, it might very well be fascinating. As one reviewer remarked, the book could find a place on the required-reading shelf for a course in the new African states. For the reader looking for the Nadine Gordimer of the deft touch and the dazzling insights, however, the relief moments are rare indeed.

Here is one, for instance. An old servant is bringing ice, complaining that Bray doesn't stay with them more:

He withheld the ice until Bray answered.

"I didn't know I was coming, Festus. I tried to phone. . . ."

The excuses were accepted and the ice put down in the convention, invented by white men long ago and become, curiously, part of the old black man's dignity, that his "master's" concerns were his own.[11]

This small, beautifully captured moment (all too rare in the novel), lifts an entire page of heavy political essay material into the vivid life we look for in Miss Gordimer's writing.

It is apropos to note that Miss Gordimer has greater success with moments left over from the colonial regime, such as this. Old traditions, relationships, traits, invariably come off better than the postindependence scene, which goes heavy-footed into polemics. But then, I suppose we should remind ourselves, Faulkner's richest writing is of the Old South, that of the Compsons and Sartorises, not of the New.

When the writing does go into the descriptive scene, political tendentiousness imprisons the writer's imagination. Consider, for instance, this quick shot at another ceremonial dinner:

The warm potato-smell and the mixture of black and white faces in the formally dressed herd pressing to the entrance were to him evidence that this was not just another municipal gathering—this was Africa, and this time Africans were honoured guests, being met with a bow and a smile. There was a satisfaction—naive, he knew; never mind—in this most obvious and, ultimately, unimportant aspect of change. It did not matter any more to the Africans whether white people wanted to dine with them or not; they themselves were now the governing elite, and the whites were the ones who had to sue for the pleasure of their company. Fifty pounds a head for a ticket; he waited in line behind a rusty-faced, bald Englishman and a lively plump Scot with their blond wives, and a black lady, probably the wife of some minor official, who had faithfully assumed their uniform of decollete and pearls. She smelled almost surgically of eau-de-Cologne. The African mayor and the white President of the Chamber of Commerce dealt jointly with the receiving lines, dispensing identical unctuousness.[12]

Except for "smelled almost surgically," which is good Gordimer, the passage is Dickensian, distinctly not *le mot juste* of Flaubert, which, with her own distinctive flavor, is Miss Gordimer's hallmark.

Part 3 of the novel takes place back in Gala. Bray sits under a fig tree writing a report—then, during a noon pause, a high-pitched distant note gives him a *déjà vu*: a car burning, bodies bleeding—a scene so vivid and arresting that his skin crawls (see final pages). He puts the disturbing vision aside and immerses himself in plans for a trade school. The clubhouse of the white colony has suitable rooms, but upon inquiry he receives a polite rebuff. The members of the Gala Club had always been willing to serve the community, but felt that the Club buildings were inappropriate and unsuitable for adult education classes. Finally, the Indian community allows him the use of Gandhi Hall. They are eager to do a favor for the government, in the hope that it will be remembered.

Bray, in his early relationship with Rebecca, had been curiously adolescent in meeting her, following that first sex in the dusky room. He hadn't known how to face her in daylight. She is the one to create ease in their meetings. The affair continues, completely lacking in passion, or in very much meaning of any sort. She is completely accommodating, undemanding, a matter-of-fact sexual partner. They have picnics together, go swimming, have sex—occasionally oral—she smokes his cigars. Discreet as they are, the affair is known, but no consequences ensue.

He gets a letter from Mweta, clearly implying that Bray is expected to keep in touch with Shinza and report on his activities. To make Bray's position even more trying, it is at this time that a new chief of police replaces the one who had imprisoned and tortured the young hitchhiker. Bray gains the reputation for having political power, but in a discomforting way. Like Greene's Scobie, he has power that he is reluctant to use. He wishes only for justice and the reconciliation of his old friends. He tries to see Shinza, but is turned back. He has more than a suspicion that Shinza is over the border recruiting a force.

Rebecca doesn't understand his hesitancy to act upon his suspicions. She would be off like a shot, she says, to inform on Shinza and consolidate his position with the government. Bray, however, is in a dilemma of loyalties that Rebecca cannot fully appreciate. Both Shinza and Mweta are old comrades in the independence struggle. Mweta, he concedes, has been embarked upon a program of accommodation, but he has an implied pledge of loyalty from Bray; while Shinza has peculiarly strong ties to Bray—in a sense, Shinza represents Bray's younger idealism about the new nation. He cannot intervene directly between these two old friends; he must help them work it out.

V *Violence Increases*

Bray is summoned to a rendezvous with Shinza, and they have a long talk, "the understanding between them of people who are both lying." Shinza is increasingly bitter about Mweta's sellout to corporate interests—the factories and mills were to be state-owned, that was the old plan. The country is still exporting an overwhelming proportion of its raw products, just as in the old days; so nothing is changed except that the masters are black. Shinza refuses to concede that he is forming an army for counterrevolution; his strategy is working through union organizations. Strikes are widespread now; the nation might very well be paralyzed by a national strike.

Bray's personal life is complicated by the appearance of Rebecca's husband; or so he anticipates. As we have seen in Miss Gordimer's management of sexual matters elsewhere, the traditional triangle of husband-wife-and-other-man never develops. The writing strategy, which Chekhov spelled out in his letters, can of course become a reverse formula for realism; that is, underplaying the reader's tradition-conditioned expectations. So it is here; Rebecca reassures Bray, and she is right. Gordon, her husband, a "small, graceful man," is on the scene for a short, pleasant stay.

Trouble begins to break out all over the province. To discourage union activism, the PIP Young Pioneers, in a variety of Red Guard violence, invade villages, intimidate people, and break heads as well as cooking pots. Strikes and lockouts spread, however; whole villages are burned and cattle slaughtered. Rebecca's husband insists that her children (we had forgotten about them, so little have we seen them) be sent south to South Africa for safety and schooling.

Part 4 of the novel is almost pure politics. The People's Independent Party Congress at the Capital is the occasion. Shinza is there, still allowed freedom in a sort of fiction of legalism. He makes a populist appeal on behalf of the farmers and workers, voicing forcefully his fear that the PIP will become a party of entrenched civil servants and bureaucrats. Although African, black autocracy is still autocracy. Mweta, charismatic as ever, warns quite directly that trade unions must not form an opposition party.

Bray, involved in one of the long arguments, tries to recall for them some of the common denominators that once held them united for the same goals:

Would you agree we've always accepted what Sartre once wrote, that socialism is the movement of man recreating himself? Whatever the paroxysms of experiment alòng the way—whether it's Robespierre or Stalin or Mao Tse-tung or Castro—it's the only way there is to go, in the sense that every other way is a way back. What do you want to see here? Another China? Another America?[13]

By the end of the Congress, Bray is recognized privately, by the new black establishment, as a "Shinza man." Back in Gala, he has another meeting with Shinza. Rebecca fears that he may be on dangerous ground, but he discounts her fears, and besides, " 'Shinza's trying to do what I believe should be done here.' "

VI The Final Violence

Shinza knows that further violence against union activities is on the way. The Young Pioneers, perhaps even mercenaries hired by the corporations, will try to bring the union membership (and hence Shinza's growing power) into submission. Shinza would like an observation team from the ILO as a possible safeguard; he proposes that Bray "visit his family" as a front, but go to Switzerland to put the case before the international labor organization. Then the whole thrust of Shinza's intention comes forth: with an international team restraining the government violence, with his force from across the border, and with his thousands of devoted union workers, he thinks he has a good chance to take over the government and put it back on the right track.

Bray has little time to turn over in his mind this daring scheme; his heart inclines toward Shinza. But it's too late; Mweta sends his Young Pioneers into Gala for a "holy burning" of huts. Even Gandhi Hall, where Bray had established his trade school goes up in flames. Bray is wounded in a violent encounter between union members and Young Pioneers. Mercenaries are in evidence, clubbing women and children.

Bray decides that he and Rebecca must leave without delay. " 'You mean you'll go to Switzerland?' " she asks. He will do what he can for Shinza, he says. Bray has "the sense of all forces disengaged and fallen apart, that he had been having all day." He is beginning, dimly, to believe that his name may be Rubashov. On the road, they are stopped at a roadblock, and as Bray is getting tools from the car, bodies burst from the tall roadside grass, and he falls under heavy blows. He hears Rebecca screaming. He tries to talk to them in Gala, but the words won't come.

In the final chapters of the book, Rebecca has the desolate task of seeing to Bray's body. Friendly villagers, who had known Bray in the years past, come to help, then friends from Gala. Apparently his assailants were miners who thought he was a white leader of mercenaries; as they were from distant areas, they did not know him. One friend expresses the fear they all acknowledge: " 'The thing is, of course, all our dear friends abroad will say he was killed by the people he loved and what else can you expect of them, and how ungrateful they are. . . .' "[14]

Rebecca goes to Switzerland to pick up money Bray had smuggled out for her, then to London. She considers going to see Bray's wife, but upon further thought, decides not to. It would only mean reliving the distress. She does meet a fellow fugitive from Africa, who hasn't heard the news. Upon learning of Bray's death, she says, " 'Of course, he was with Shinza and that crowd. Poor devil. These nice white liberals getting mixed up in things they don't understand. What did he expect?' "[15]

Thus, Bray's name remains under one cloud or another, even

with the Shinza followers, for it was not clearly established what he was doing on that road, whether he was on his way to Mweta or on a mission to buy arms for Shinza. Mweta, with his astute sense of the power of myth, makes his own decision. When the new governmental plan for educational reform is published, he calls it "The Bray Report." Our final word comes from England:

> In a number devoted to "The Decline of Liberalism," in an English monthly journal he was discussed as an interesting case in point: a man who had "passed over from the skepticism and resignation of empirical liberalism to become one of those who are so haunted by the stupidities and evils in human affairs that they are prepared to accept apocalyptic solutions, made through blood if need be, to bring real change."[16]

Read for idea content alone (relatively easy to do, since the essay quotient of the novel is quite high), the novel reveals a stubborn and somewhat outmoded liberalism, with the dream of socialism—if we are to take Bray's ideas seriously—still overriding the hard facts of human nature. As several reviewers remarked, there is nothing factually new in the book to anyone who has followed the news from Africa. Then why write the book? It does seem in many of its pages to content itself with reportorial authenticity, forgetting for long periods the developing web of relationships which give pace and direction to a novel—and which keep the reader turning the pages.

The answer seems to be that for Miss Gordimer, the developments she chronicled were dismaying; scales fell from her eyes, and she wanted to share her discoveries with others whom, she felt, would also find them vitally important and interesting. She sensed—perhaps rightly so—that many others like herself were also dismayed to find that blacks also are corrupted by power, that they murder to maintain dominion, that the white master is replaced by an even more ruthless black master. Perhaps many others are dismayed to find that the outlets for political power implicit in Marxism—particularly those outlets made easily available by the parliamentary system as practiced in Africa—the beautiful responsiveness and flexibility of the system in English hands becomes apparatus for suppressing the opposition, for creating a one-party police state, for control of the press, and other ugly manifestations of fascism—as Miss Gordimer's novel so ably delineates. It is dismaying, I suppose, to discover that English traits—respect for the loyal opposition, regard for the proprieties, for "what one does" in the civic consciousness—are absolutely essential for the proper functioning of that sophisticated political instrument. Of course, South Africa pioneered in the demonstration of how the English system could easily be converted into a one-party oligarchy. So, in a theoretical sense, the South Africans reared in an English tradition, of which Miss Gordimer is one, should have been prepared for this phenomenon of political change. South African students of Africa should not have been too surprised at what happened in country after country after independence. Even tribal genocide in the name of political necessity.

Political reportage aside, the novel when read for signs of the novelist's art is disappointing. It is Miss Gordimer's *Nostromo*. That is, it smells of the study, of a vast and often joyless effort to manipulate huge quantities of material without losing narrative flow. One can sense the mind hard at work, erecting adversary situations that will illuminate political facts, aligning patterns of stress—in short, creating plot. And with every "plotty" invention, we move further from the Nadine Gordimer who charmed us in the short stories. A sense of wearying effort pervades the slow trend of events; and virtually every novelistic gambit violates the Gordimer creative profile that we have been discovering and celebrating throughout this study. The dramatist, not the poet, is at work here. In place of dazzling image, epiphany, inductive movement of situation, *traits de lumière*, and other enchanting arts we have observed, we have political conspiracy, plotting, hard dramatic encounter, and all heavy, heavy of foot.

Conclusion

AS this study concludes with a perusal of the novels, which I regard as relative failures—relative only to the brilliance of the superb short stories—perhaps it should be the business of these final lines to restore some of the balance that may have been mislaid because of rhetorical arrangements in these pages.

The best of Miss Gordimer's short stories—and any reader who has reached this point should be able to come up with my list—rank with the best of Chekhov, Katherine Mansfield, Hemingway, James Joyce's *Dubliners*; indeed, they rank with the finest of their kind, to put my judgment in absolute terms. They have universal appeal, even though they arise from the African scene. They are not "about" Africa, but are about love denied where love is most difficult but desperately needed. They are about the violations of love, about injury to one not truly loved enough. They are about undeserved love, given from simple hearts but falling upon the ground of pseudosophistication, barren and unresponsive. And of course, the love, pity, compassion evoked by the stories emerge from the dazzling imagery of sky and veld to support with poetic intensity the perceptions of situation.

The novels are something else. Frequently, the trouble is that in seeking a more sustained story structure, Miss Gordimer is drawn into the sort of direct racial confrontation that she avoided in her most successful short stories. Perhaps the nature of the problem, as defined in the vocabulary of the social studies, insists upon such confrontation and plot situations. The stereotypes of the traditional black status are succeeded by the stereotypes offered by sociology for the new status. Either one is bad medicine for a writer of Miss Gordimer's capabilities.

How does such characterization compare with what we find in previous, enduring writers? I have never found, in fiction, a finer creation of the black man than Conrad's James Wait; nor

161

in drama than Shakespeare's Othello. In both instances, be it noted, the author immerses his black man in a complex tangle of universal human concerns, instead of giving him the simplistic and sentimental role of the victim—which, we may note, denies him his humanity. Othello's new marriage and consequently easily aroused jealousy, his pride in his military prowess and his ability to command, and so on through other facets of man's being, are all examples of this. In the same way James Wait's condescending arrogance, so beautifully realized by Conrad, or his self-deceptive fraud, illustrate these concerns. They are superb human beings, "authors of their woe," appealingly flawed. Few modern literary blacks, struggling in the muck of their authors' sociological jargon, have such fortune.

If race is the only story worthy of the sustained attention of the South African novelist, then we must offer him our sympathy. We hope for more—and Miss Gordimer in her short stories has nourished that hope. Actually, race may not be the dominant social issue at all; many South Africans will insist that the battle is between whites and whites—whites of English descent versus whites of Dutch descent.

Finally, let us acknowledge that remarkably few masters of the short story form exhibit a comparable mastery of the novel. Many of the finest never tried: Chekhov, Katherine Mansfield, Poe, Maupassant, O. Henry, Saki. Katherine Anne Porter, after twenty years of effort, produced *Ship of Fools*, and few would agree that it was worth the effort. It is a tedious bore, with a few flashes of short story brilliance inserted. Hemingway comes to mind as a possible exception; yet his novels are merely competent. He would not have been awarded the Nobel Prize for his novels, nor would he have found a place in university courses devoted to modern fiction. His short stories put their stamp upon a generation of writers, and it is as a short story writer that his name will be recorded in literary histories. His novels have quite conventional content and structure, quite distinct from his brilliant short-story forms. They are readable, they are good Hollywood; but they are undistinguished. Hollywood has never captured "A Clean Well-lighted Place," "Hills like White Elephants," or "In Another Country."

Similarly with Miss Gordimer. I can see a Hollywood production of *A Guest of Honour*, done with serious attention to locale and political commentary, in the manner of *The Ugly American* or *For Whom the Bell Tolls*. The movie would cause a small ripple, then disappear, to reappear in a year or so on the late TV screen.

This is not true of her short stories, the half-dozen of her best, with hopefully more to come. The opalescent magic of "Is There Nowhere Else Where We Can Meet?" will defy time and translation. That one, plus a few more, puts Miss Gordimer securely among the masters, and she shines with a luster equal to theirs.

Notes and References

Chapter One

1. "The Train from Rhodesia," *The Soft Voice of the Serpent* (New York: The Viking Press, 1950), p. 48.
2. "Is There Nowhere Else Where We Can Meet?" *The Soft Voice of the Serpent*, p. 92.
3. "A Bit of Young Life," *Six Feet of the Country* (New York: Simon & Schuster, 1956), p. 41.
4. *Ibid.*, p. 55.
5. *Ibid.*, p. 57.
6. "A Style of Her Own," *Friday's Footprint* (New York: The Viking Press. 1960), p. 67.
7. *Ibid.*, p. 70.
8. "Check Yes or No," *Ibid.*, p. 93.
9. *Ibid.*, p. 103.
10. *Ibid.*, p. 105.
11. "The Catch," *The Soft Voice of the Serpent*, p. 8.
12. "The Amateurs," *Ibid.*, p. 97.
13. "The Catch," *The Soft Voice of the Serpent*, p. 10.
14. *Ibid.*, p. 11.
15. *Ibid.*, p. 13.
16. *Ibid.*, p. 18.
17. *Ibid.*, pp. 24–25.
18. Nadine Gordimer, *Livingstone's Companions* (New York: The Viking Press, 1971).
19. "Why Haven't You Written?" *Ibid.*, p. 219.
20. *Ibid.*, p. 231.
21. "No Place Like," *Ibid.*, p. 183.
22. "Livingstone's Companions," *Ibid.*, p. 3.
23. *Ibid.*, pp. 36–37.
24. Seán O'Faoláin, *Short Stories, A Study in Pleasure* (Boston: Little, Brown & Co.), p. 94.
25. *Ibid.*, p. 95.

Chapter Two

1. "Oh, Woe is Me," *The Soft Voice of the Serpent*, p. 133.
2. *Ibid.*, p. 142.

3. *Ibid.*, p. 222.
4. *Ibid.*, p. 207.
5. *Ibid.*, p. 208.
6. *Ibid.*, p. 218.
7. *Six Feet of the Country*, p. 1.
8. *Ibid.*, p. 14.
9. *Ibid.*, p. 5.
10. *Ibid.*, p. 69.
11. *Ibid.*, p. 71.
12. *Ibid.*, p. 78.
13. *Ibid.*, p. 84.
14. *Ibid.*, p. 73.
15. *The Soft Voice of the Serpent*, p. 97.
16. *Ibid.*, p. 99.
17. *Ibid.*, p. 104.
18. *Ibid.*, p. 106.
19. *Six Feet of the Country*, p. 151.
20. *Ibid.*, p. 167.
21. *Ibid.*, p. 153.
22. *Ibid.*, p. 154.
23. *Ibid.*, p. 156.
24. *Ibid.*, p. 185.
25. *Ibid.*, p. 185.
26. *Ibid.*, p. 186.
27. *Ibid.*, p. 201.
28. *Ibid.*, p. 204.

Chapter Three

1. "The Defeated," *The Soft Voice of the Serpent*, p. 194.
2. *Ibid.*, p. 194.
3. *Ibid.*, p. 196.
4. *Ibid.*, p. 198.
5. *Ibid.*, p. 201.
6. *Ibid.*, pp. 202–3.
7. *Ibid.*, p. 212.
8. "The Umbilical Cord," *The Soft Voice of the Serpent*, p. 160.
9. *Ibid.*, p. 165.
10. *Ibid.*
11. "Charmed Lives," *Six Feet of the Country*, p. 169.
12. *Ibid.*, p. 173.
13. *Ibid.*
14. *Ibid.*, p. 181.
15. *Ibid.*, p. 182.

16. "The Prisoner," *The Soft Voice of the Serpent*, p. 26.

17. *Ibid.*, p. 78.

18. *Ibid.*, p. 83.

19. *Ibid.*, p. 89.

20. *Ibid.*, pp. 89–90.

21. *Ibid.*, pp. 90–91.

22. "La Vie Boheme," *The Soft Voice of the Serpent*, p. 119.

23. *Ibid.*, p. 122.

24. *Ibid.*, p. 124.

25. *Ibid.*, p. 132.

26. "A Watcher of the Dead," *The Soft Voice of the Serpent*, p. 56.

27. *Ibid.*, p. 59.

28. *Ibid.*, pp. 62–63.

29. *Ibid.*, p. 67.

30. "The Kindest Things to Do," *The Soft Voice of the Serpent*, p. 26.

31. *Ibid.*, pp. 26–27.

32. *Ibid.*, pp. 30–31.

33. *Ibid.*, p. 32.

34. *Ibid.*, p. 33.

35. *Ibid.*, p. 33.

36. Katherine Mansfield, *Stories* (New York: Vintage Books, 1956), pp. 323–24.

37. "Tenants of the Last Tree House," *Not for Publication* (New York: The Viking Press, 1965), p. 147.

38. *Ibid.*, p. 164.

39. *Ibid.*, p. 165.

40. "Another Part of the Sky," *The Soft Voice of the Serpent*, p. 144.

41. *Ibid.*, p. 155.

42. *Ibid.*, pp. 154–55.

43. "The Hour and the Years," *The Soft Voice of the Serpent*, p. 34.

44. *Ibid.*, p. 46.

45. *Ibid.*, p. 47.

Chapter Four

1. "Our Bovary," *Friday's Footprint* (New York: The Viking Press, 1960), p. 146.

2. *Ibid.*, p. 161.

3. "An Image of Success," *Friday's Footprint*, p. 202.

4. *Ibid.*, p. 211.

5. *Ibid.*, p. 221.

6. *Ibid.*, p. 233.

7. "Out of Season," *Six Feet of the Country* (New York: Simon & Schuster, 1956), p. 87.

8. *Ibid.*, p. 88.

9. *Ibid.*, p. 90.

10. *Ibid.*, p. 95.

11. "The White Goddess and the Mealie Question," *Six Feet of the Country*, p. 115.

12. *Ibid.*, p. 120.

13. "Face from Atlantis," *Six Feet of the Country*, p. 17.

14. *Ibid.*, p. 26.

15. *Ibid.*, p. 30.

16. *Ibid.*, p. 34.

17. *Ibid.*

18. *Ibid.*, p. 37.

19. *Ibid.*, p. 38.

20. *Ibid.*, p. 39.

Chapter Five

1. *The Lying Days* (New York: Simon & Schuster, 1953).

2. *Ibid.*, p. 167.

3. *Ibid.*, p. 8.

4. *Ibid.*, p. 14.

5. *Ibid.*, p. 70.

6. *Ibid.*, p. 85.

7. *Ibid.*, p. 170.

8. *Ibid.*, p. 207.

9. *Ibid.*, p. 251.

10. *Ibid.*, pp. 275–76.

Chapter Six

1. *A World of Strangers* (New York: Simon & Schuster, 1958).

2. *Ibid.*, p. iv.

3. *Ibid.*, p. 24.

4. *Ibid.*, p. 39.

5. *Ibid.*, p. 50.

6. *Ibid.*, p. 53.

7. *Ibid.*, pp. 56–57.

8. *Ibid.*, p. 99.

9. *Ibid.*, p. 100.

10. *Ibid.*, p. 109.

11. *Ibid.*, p. 134.

12. *Ibid.*, pp. 144–45.

13. *Ibid.*, p. 150.
14. *Ibid.*, p. 154.
15. *Ibid.*, p. 170.
16. *Ibid.*, p. 177.
17. *Ibid.*, p. 189.
18. *Ibid.*, p. 311.

Chapter Seven

1. *Occasion for Loving* (New York: Viking Press, 1963).
2. *Ibid.*, p. 23.
3. *Ibid.*, p. 3.
4. *Ibid.*, p. 5.
5. *Ibid.*, p. 8.
6. *Ibid.*, p. 15.
7. *Ibid.*, pp. 41–42.
8. *Ibid.*, p. 52.
9. *Ibid.*, p. 53.
10. *Ibid.*
11. *Ibid.*, p. 59.
12. *Ibid.*, p. 78.
13. *Ibid.*, p. 81.
14. *Ibid.*, pp. 84–85.
15. *Ibid.*, pp. 106–107.
16. *Ibid.*, p. 129.
17. *Ibid.*, p. 164.
18. *Ibid.*, p. 171.
19. *Ibid.*, p. 176.
20. *Ibid.*, pp. 182–83.
21. *Ibid.*, pp. 213–14.
22. *Ibid.*, p. 218.
23. *Ibid.*, p. 224.
24. *Ibid.*, p. 290.
25. *Ibid.*, pp. 296–97.
26. *The English Novel in South Africa* (Cape Town: N.U.S.A.S., 1960), p. 18.

Chapter Eight

1. *The Late Bourgeois World* (New York: The Viking Press, 1966).
2. *Ibid.*, p. 49.
3. *Ibid.*, p. 39.
4. *Ibid.*, p. 45.

5. *Ibid.*, pp. 26–27.
6. *Ibid.*, pp. 30–31.
7. *Ibid.*, p. 28.
8. *Ibid.*, p. 76.
9. *Ibid.*, pp. 83–84.
10. *Ibid.*, p. 100.
11. *Ibid.*, p. 109.

Chapter Nine

1. *A Guest of Honour* (New York: The Viking Press, 1970).
2. *Ibid.*, p. 7.
3. *Ibid.*, p. 12.
4. *Ibid.*, p. 24.
5. *Ibid.*, p. 25.
6. *Ibid.*, p. 61.
7. *Ibid.*, pp. 81–82.
8. *Ibid.*, p. 83.
9. *Ibid.*, p. 95.
10. *Ibid.*, p. 96.
11. *Ibid.*, p. 178.
12. *Ibid.*, p. 191.
13. *Ibid.*, p. 380.
14. *Ibid.*, p. 479.
15. *Ibid.*, p. 502.
16. *Ibid.*, p. 503.

Selected Bibliography

PRIMARY SOURCES

1. Short Story Collections

Face to Face. Johannesburg: Silver Leaf Books, 1949.

The Soft Voice of the Serpent. New York: Simon & Schuster, 1952.
This first collection published in New York omits three stories in *Face to Face*: "The Battlefield at No. 29," "The Last of the Old-fashioned Girls," and "No Luck Tonight." Added are eight stories not in *Face to Face*: "The Catch," "The Hour and the Years," "A Watcher of the Dead," "Treasures of the Sea," "The Prisoner," "Another Part of the Sky," "The End of the Tunnel," and "The Defeated."

The Soft Voice of the Serpent. New York: New American Library, 1956.

The Soft Voice of the Serpent. New York: The Viking Press (Compass Books), 1962.

Six Feet of the Country. London: Gollancz, Ltd., 1956.

Six Feet of the Country. New York: Simon & Schuster, 1956. The New York edition has an additional story, "The White Goddess and the Mealie Question," not found in the London edition.

Friday's Footprint. London: Gollancz, Ltd., 1960.

Friday's Footprint. New York: The Viking Press, 1960. The London edition has "Something for the Time Being," not found in the New York edition. One of the stories, "An Image of Success," might more properly be described as a novella.

Not for Publication. New York: The Viking Press, 1965.

Livingstone's Companions. New York: The Viking Press, 1971.

2. Novels

The Lying Days. New York: Simon & Schuster, 1953.

A World of Strangers. New York: Simon & Schuster, 1958.

Occasion for Loving. New York: The Viking Press, 1963.

The Late Bourgeois World. New York: The Viking Press, 1966.

A Guest of Honour. New York: The Viking Press, 1970.

3. Other Writings: Essays, Reviews, Published Lectures

"Johannesburg" *Holiday*, 18 (August, 1955), 46–51.

"Apartheid" *Holiday*, 25 (April, 1959), 94–95.

171

"The English Novel in South Africa" *N.U.S.A.S.*, 1960, pp. 16–21. A
   lecture delivered in July, 1959 at the Winter School of the Na-
   tional Union of South African Students, at the Witwatersrand
   University, Johannesburg.
"Leaving School" *The London Magazine* (N.S.) III (2) (May, 1963),
   59–65.
"Censored, Banned, Gagged" *Encounter* 20 (June, 1963), 59–63.
"Party of One" *Holiday* 34 (July, 1963), 12–17.
"The Interpreters: Some Themes and Directions in African Literature"
   The Kenyon Review 32 (Issue 1, 1970), 9–26.
"Themes and Attitudes in African Literature" *Michigan Quarterly
   Review* IX (Fall, 1970), 221–31. A Lecture delivered at the
   Avery Hopwood Awards, University of Michigan, April, 1970.
"The Life of Accra, the Flowers of Abidjan: a West African Diary"
   Atlantic Monthly 228 (November, 1971), 85–89.
"Tanzania" *Atlantic Monthly* 231 (May, 1973), 8–18.

SECONDARY SOURCES

BALLIETT, WHITNEY, "Review of *A World of Strangers.*" *New Yorker*,
   November 29, 1958.
BARKHAM, JOHN, "The Author" *Saturday Review of Literature* 46
   (January 12, 1963), 63.
BLAIR, ALISON, "Review of *The Lying Days*" *Encounter* 2 (1) (Jan-
   uary, 1954), 74–77.
FEINSTEIN, ELAINE, "Nadine Gordimer." *London Magazine* (August–
   September, 1972), pp. 159–60.
NELL, RACILIA JILIAN, *Nadine Gordimer: Novelist and Short Story
   Writer: A Bibliography of her Works and Selected Criticism.*
   Johannesburg: University of the Witwatersrand, 1964. The most
   complete bibliography to 1963.
SHEPPARD, R. Z., "Review of *A Guest of Honour.*" *Time Magazine*
   (November 16, 1970), pp. 100–101.
SHRAPNEL, NORMAN, "Review of *A Guest of Honour.*" *Manchester
   Guardian Weekly* (May 8, 1971), p. 19.
ULMAN, RUTH, "Nadine Gordimer." *Wilson Library Bulletin* 33 (May,
   1959), 616.
WEEKS, EDWARD, "Review of *Friday's Footprint.*" *Atlantic Monthly*
   205 (January, 1960), 547–48.
WYNDHAM, FRANCIS. "Review of *Six Feet of the Country.*" *London
   Magazine*, III (August, 1956), 67–69. "Review of *A World of
   Strangers*" *London Magazine*, V (July, 1958), 71–72.

Index

173